The Big Band Reader
Songs Favored by Swing Era Orchestras and Other Popular Ensembles

William E. Studwell
Mark Baldin

The Haworth Press®
New York • London • Oxford

The Haworth Press, Inc., 10 Alice Street, Binghamton, NY 13904-1580

Cover design by Marylouise E. Doyle.

Library of Congress Cataloging-in-Publication Data

Studwell, William E. (William Emmett), 1936-
    The big band reader : songs favored by swing era orchestras and other popular ensembles / William E. Studwell, Mark Baldin.
        p.   cm.
    Includes bibliographical references (p.   ) and indexes.
    ISBN 0-7890-0914-5 (hard : alk. paper)—ISBN 0-7890-0915-3 (pbk. : alk. paper)
    1. Big band music—History and criticism. 2. Swing (Music)—History and criticism. I. Baldin, Mark. II. Title.

ML3518 .S83 2000
784.4'81654—dc21

99-462194

Words can be birds
In open sky,
That meet a beat
And yet still fly;
And if aloft
For very long,
They make a flight
We call a song.

ABOUT THE AUTHORS

William E. Studwell, MA, MSLS, is Professor and Principal Cataloger at the University Libraries of Northern Illinois University in DeKalb, and the author of *Barbershops, Bullets, and Ballads: An Annotated Anthology of Underappreciated American Musical Jewels, 1865-1918; College Fight Songs: An Annotated Anthology; Publishing Glad Tidings: Essays on Christmas Music;* and *State Songs of the United States: An Annotated Anthology* (The Haworth Press, Inc.). Mr. Studwell is the author of nineteen other books on music, including reference books on popular songs, national songs, Christmas songs, ballets, and operas. He has also written three books on cataloging and almost 340 articles on library science and music. A nationally known expert on carols, college fight songs, and Library of Congress subject headings, he has made approximately 425 radio, television, and print appearances in national, regional, and local media.

Mark Baldin is the principal trumpet player with the Rockford Symphony in Rockford, Illinois. He has played with various ensembles in the northern Illinois region, including a long-standing big band in DeKalb, Illinois. Mr. Baldin is also a private music teacher and is currently a morning radio personality for WLBK in DeKalb, Illinois.

CONTENTS

SOME UNHERALDED BANDS

Preface

In London, "Big Ben" makes famous sounds every quarter of an hour. In the United States, big bands made famous sounds for about a quarter of a century. From the late 1920s to the early 1950s, big bands dominated the American popular music scene. These bands, and much of their music, are largely a thing of the past now, despite some revivals and the continuance of some of the bands under the old names, obviously, with new personnel. To honor the music of these very popular ensembles, this volume presents over 140 essays on the themes, preferred numbers, and top songs of about seventy big bands that were in existence by the early 1960s. The themes and favorite numbers of dozens of other bands are also tangentially or indirectly mentioned in the text or in the supplementary appendix.

Arranged in three broad sections, *The Better-Known Swing Bands* (ensembles favoring the jazz variant that encouraged dancing), *The Sweet Bands* (ensembles favoring softer, more sentimental numbers), and *Some Unheralded Bands* (good ensembles not receiving much attention or not having a big-name leader), the various orchestras are listed alphabetically by the first name of the bandleader. For example, the Artie Shaw Orchestra is listed under "Artie" rather than under "Shaw." This reflects the usual pattern of referring to the bands as, for example, the "Count Basie Orchestra" or the "Tommy Dorsey Orchestra." Minor semantic variations such as "with the Orchestra" or "and his Orchestra" are ignored here. All ensembles with a personal name and the word orchestra in their titles will be written with the clear and consistent pattern "[name] Orchestra," for instance, the "Ben Bernie Orchestra." Other semantic patterns, such as "Guy Lombardo and his Royal Canadians" are given in their most common natural patterns.

Each of the bands will be covered by one to four essays relating to their favorite numbers. Those essays will focus on the bands and their music, with passing references to bands and persons not featured in this volume and various other asides of potential interest. The quantity of preferred-song essays included for an individual band depends substantially on the importance of the group. Other factors, however, such as the amount of interesting information available and the complexity of the history of the songs involved, help to determine the extent of historical coverage in each case.

All such judgments, including which bands to include in which group or which bands to exclude entirely, were based on the joint research and knowledge of the authors. Mark Baldin is an accomplished performer in several types of orchestras as well as a radio personality, and William Studwell has written extensively about American popular music. Among his writings are *The Popular Song Reader* (1994), which in a different way covers some of the songs mentioned here, and *The Americana Song Reader* (1997), which occasionally makes reference to numbers noted in this volume.

As in the aforementioned volumes and others in the "reader" series, the essays on the numbers are crafted in a style intended to not only inform but also entertain. This pattern of readable reference books is intended to bring out the best in the topic covered. In the present volume, which gives retrospective tribute to the big bands so prominent in twentieth-century American popular culture, the authors hope to present an accurate and lively picture of these artistic groups. So, without any more delay, let us, in the words of Ira Gershwin, "Strike Up the Band!"

THE BETTER-KNOWN SWING BANDS

ARTIE SHAW
(THE ARTIE SHAW ORCHESTRA, 1937-1939, 1940-1955)

Begin the Beguine

By a lucky accident, the chronicling of big band numbers in this volume begins with "Begin the Beguine." The three-part tale of "Beguine" began in 1935 with *Jubilee,* a musical by the outstanding composer and lyricist Cole Porter (1891-1964). Although Porter, from a rich Indiana family, was for years considered just a dilettante dabbling in music, he had firmly established himself as a top creator of musicals by 1934 after one of his best shows, *Anything Goes,* appeared on Broadway. *Anything Goes,* which included four notable numbers, "Blow, Gabriel, Blow," "I Get a Kick Out of You," "You're the Top," and "Anything Goes," was a better show overall than *Jubilee* the following year. Yet *Jubilee* had two very good pieces, the standard "Just One of Those Things" and the now classic "Begin the Beguine."

"Beguine," the musical portrayal of a South American bolero-style dance, was not an immediate hit. This was due in part to the unusual length of the original number. By 1938 composer and arranger Jerry Gray had altered the length of "Beguine" and produced an excellent arrangement of the composition. (Later on, Gray would be closely associated with the Glenn Miller Orchestra, including helping to lead it after Miller's premature death.)

Gray's revised score was the magic ingredient to turn "Beguine" into a huge hit. The Artie Shaw Orchestra recorded Porter's masterpiece in July 1936. The rendition, with Shaw (1910-   ) on the lead clarinet, was such a sensation that, for a while, Shaw's reputation as a swing bandleader rivaled that of the great Benny Goodman. Although the flash of success created by "Beguine" was more than Shaw could handle, "Beguine" instantly became the theme song of the various ensembles headed by him. He very capably recorded other classics, such as "Stardust" (1927, music by Hoagy Carmichael, lyrics added in 1929 by Mitchell Parish) and "Dancing in the Dark" (1931, words by Howard Dietz, music by Arthur Schwartz), yet Shaw and "Beguine" were almost inseparable. As another Shaw favorite, "Day In—Day Out" (1939, by Johnny Mercer and Rube Bloom), suggested, "Beguine" was associated with Shaw day after day, night after night.

Frenesi

Artie Shaw, born Arthur Arshawsky in New York City in 1910, is known for several things. He was the leader of one of the top swing bands, a clarinetist of note, a composer of consequence, and was often married. His numerous wives included the beautiful actresses Lana Turner and Ava Gardner plus Betty Kern, the daughter of another famous musician, Jerome Kern. These marriages, chronicled in Shaw's 1952 autobiography *The Trouble with Cinderella,* kept Shaw in the news perhaps as often as did the accomplishments of the Artie Shaw Orchestra. Shaw's autobiography reflected Shaw's far-from-ideal love life, a definite contrast to the fairy-tale *Cinderella* fantasy.

With this background in mind, it is fascinating to note that one of Shaw's favorite numbers was the lively and playful "Frenesi." Meaning "frenzy," "folly," or "madness" in Spanish, "Frenesi" was created in 1939. Alberto Dominguez wrote both the music and the original Spanish words, with an English translation written some years later by the noted singer, pianist, and composer Ray Charles, along with Sidney Keith Russell (also known as Bob Russell). Another well-known song by Dominguez, interestingly, was "Perfidia" (1941), cowritten with Milton Leeds. "Perfidia" means "unfaithful" or "treacherous" in Spanish.

With his marital difficulties and periodic disgust with, and retirement from, music, Shaw understandably did not embrace another Spanish-titled song of the period, "Amor" (meaning "love"). Created in 1944 by musician Gabriel Ruiz and lyricist Ricardo López Méndez, the English words for upbeat "Amor" were, appropriately, crafted by a person with an equally upbeat name, Sunny Skylar.

Summit Ridge Drive

"Summit Ridge Drive" sounds like a street in an upscale housing subdivision. It does not sound like the name of a musical composition, much less one of some consequence. Yet, such a piece, created by Artie Shaw in 1944, and recorded by his Gramercy 5 combo, was a hit and one of Shaw's favorites. Although far from a classic, it was certainly good enough to motivate Will Hudson, a composer of some repute, to create a special arrangement of "Summit" the same year.

One of the more significant contributions to the "fox-trot" dance style that surfaced around 1912, "Summit" was one of several good pieces written by Shaw. Another one, "Nightmare" (1937), was a continuing favorite and was at one time Shaw's theme. An interesting companion to "Nightmare" was the song on the flip side of the 1937 recording by Shaw's New Music group. A jazz version of the British classic "It's a Long, Long Way to Tipperary" (1912, by Jack Judge and Harry Williams) was the disc mate to "Nightmare." It was all probably pure coincidence that the composition of "Tipperary," the commencement of the fox trot-mode, and Shaw's birth were around the same time, and that "Tipperary" was a favorite during the "nightmare" of World War I.

Also surely coincidence, in light of Shaw's multiple marriages, were the following musical events: Shaw and Teddy McRae wrote "Traffic Jam" (1939); Shaw and Charlie Shavers wrote "Pastel Blue" (1939), which changed to "Why Begin Again?" in 1943 when lyrics were added by Don Raye; and Shaw wrote the music for "Love of My Life" (1940), with lyrics, and therefore the title, by someone else, in this case the great Johnny Mercer. In addition, yet another coincidence was that another song had the title "Love of My Life," which was created by Cole Porter for the 1948 musical *The Pirate*. Porter, curiously, was the composer of Shaw's theme and greatest hit, "Begin the Beguine" (1935, recorded 1936).

BENNY GOODMAN
(THE BENNY GOODMAN
ORCHESTRA, 1934-1950)

And the Angels Sing

Although the title sounds like an afterthought, "And the Angels Sing" (1939) was a terrific big band number as well as a top favorite of the Benny Goodman Orchestra. Melodic and sweeping "Angels" was written by the great lyricist and competent composer Johnny Mercer, with trumpet player Ziggy Elman. (The song was later adopted as the theme of the Ziggy Elman Orchestra.) Mercer (1909-1976) also created another top Goodman number, the taunting "Goody, Goody" (1936), with Matt Malneck.

Malneck did not write much else of note, but did collaborate on the dreamy ballad "Shangri-la" (1946) with Robert Maxwell. A few years later Maxwell linked up with another songwriter, Carl Sigman, to produce the enduring standard "Ebb Tide" (1953). This three "M" sequence (Mercer, Malneck, and Maxwell) reached from 1936 to 1953.

Along with the three Ms, there were three As achieving great success during about the same period. These three As were the famous Andrews Sisters, who were the dominant female vocal group before, during, and after World War II. The song that launched the career of the Andrews Sisters was the 1937 smash hit "Bei Mir Bist Du Schoen." The songwriting team of Sammy Cahn (born Samuel Cohen) and Saul Chaplin (born Saul Kaplan) heard a very compelling Yiddish song in 1936. Not long after, Cahn devised English lyrics and Chaplin adapted the music, creating the strange, yet charming, Yiddish-English novelty that became the rage when the three Andrews angels sang.

"Bei Mir" was also performed at Carnegie Hall in New York by virtuoso clarinetist Goodman. A stickler for perfection, Goodman is reported to have said that if he missed practicing one day, he knew it, and if he didn't practice for two days, his audiences knew it. Goodman also knew, as stated in an old joke, that practice, practice, practice is how you get to Carnegie Hall.

Let's Dance

In the late 1930s, bandleader and clarinetist Benny Goodman led his orchestra in a regular series of broadcasts on the National Broadcasting Company's radio network. The title of the program was "Let's Dance," named after Goodman's theme. That number was written by lyricists Joseph Bonine and Gregory Stone and musician Fanny Baldridge in 1935, with the melody derived from the waltz section of "Invitation to the Dance" (1819), by German classical composer Carl Maria von Weber (1786-1826).

These broadcasts, several movies, many recordings, and countless performances before live audiences, using "Let's Dance" and the rest of the brilliant repertory of the Benny Goodman Orchestra, motivated millions of Americans to dance for decades. Among the pieces in the repertory were several by Chicago-born Benjamin David Goodman (1909-1986), often called the "king of swing." Perhaps his best number was "Stompin' at the Savoy" (1936), an instrumental with Edgar Sampson and Chick Webb. Although "Stompin'" caused a lot of foot movement without a set of lyrics to accompany it, Andy Razaf wrote some after-the-melody words for the swing classic.

Other compositions by Goodman include the following: another top Goodman hit, "Don't Be That Way" (1938), words by Mitchell Parish, music by Goodman and Sampson; "Flying Home" (1939), words by Sid Robin, music by Goodman and Lionel Hampton; "Lullaby in Rhythm" (1938), words and music by Goodman, Sampson, Clarence Prift, and Walter Hirsch; "Georgia Jubilee" (1934), by Goodman and Arthur Schutt; "Swingtime in the Rockies" (1936), by Goodman and Jimmy Mundy; "Life Goes to a Party" (1937), by Goodman and Harry James; "A Home in the Clouds" (1939), by Benny Carter and Goodman; "Air Mail Special" (1941), by Goodman, Mundy, and Charlie Christian; "Two O'Clock Jump" (1941), by James, Count Basie, and Goodman; "Solo Flight"

(1944), by Christian, Mundy, and Goodman; "Soft Winds" (1940), words by Fred Royal, music by Goodman; and "If Dreams Come True" (1962), by Irving Mills, Goodman, and Sampson. Goodman's close associate Sampson also created "Blue Lou" (1933) with Mills. So Goodman's ensemble performed the blues, soft songs, lullabies, rhythmic numbers, pieces that soared, love ballads, romping, stomping rousers, and jazzed-up waltzes. With such a broad selection and considerable technical competence by the orchestra (and the clarinetist who led the group), it is no wonder that Benny Goodman had few peers during the swing era.

Moonglow

In 1609, English explorer Henry Hudson made a historic voyage to North America in a ship called the "Half Moon." In 1934, American composer and future bandleader Will Hudson (1908-) made an artistic voyage toward fame when he wrote half of a song about a glowing "moon." Although Henry's trip was highly successful, resulting in, among other things, an important river being named after him, Will's cocreation of "Moonglow" (1934), collaboration on some other songs, and leadership of a band resulted in only a slight bit of fame.

"Moonglow," written with lyricists Irving Mills and Eddie De-Lange (1904-1949), was the top song by Hudson, one of the several top songs by Mills, and one of the two top songs by DeLange. It, along with another moon song, "How High the Moon" (1940, by lyricist Nancy Hamilton and composer Morgan Lewis), was one of the favorite numbers of the Benny Goodman Orchestra. (DeLange at one time led an orchestra with Hudson.) Hudson also produced the following numbers: "Jazznocracy" (1934), "White Heat" (1934), and "Eight Bars in Search of a Melody" (1936), all three without lyrics; "The Organ Grinder's Swing" (1936), with lyricists Mitchell Parish and Mills; and "Sophisticated Swing" (1936), with Parish. "Sophisticated" was the theme of the Freddy Nagel Orchestra and the Les Elgart Orchestra. (Another Elgart theme was "Heart of My Heart" [1926], by Ben Ryan.) "Sophisticated," "Eight Bars," and "Organ Grinder's" were all recorded by the Hudson-DeLange Orchestra, with "Eight Bars" the theme of the Will Hudson Orchestra. Mills also created a number of good numbers with Duke Ellington and others.

DeLange's other big hit was "A String of Pearls" (1942), written with composer Jerry Gray. DeLange also collaborated on "Along the Navajo Trail" (1945), words and music by DeLange, Dick Charles, and Larry Markes; "And So Do I" (1940), words and

music by DeLange, Stephan Weiss, and Paul Mann; "Do You Know
What It Means to Miss New Orleans?" (1946), words by DeLange,
music by Louis Alter; "Haunting Me" (1934), words by DeLange,
music by Josef Myrow; "I Wish I Were Twins" (1934), words and
music by DeLange, Frank Loesser, and Joseph Meyer; "If I'm
Lucky" (1946), words by DeLange, music by Myrow; "Solitude"
(1934), words by DeLange and Mills, music by Duke Ellington;
and "This Is Worth Fighting For" (1942), words and music by
DeLange and Sam H. Stept.

With yet another collaborator, Jimmy Van Heusen, DeLange
wrote two dream songs and two heaven songs. The song-writing
pair were "Deep in a Dream" in 1938, but said "Darn That Dream"
a bit later in 1939. Although they claimed "Heaven Can Wait" in
1939, they were immersed in the delights of "All This and Heaven
Too" just one year later in 1940. Three years earlier, composer Max
Steiner had already used "All This and Heaven Too" for the title of
his 1937 instrumental that would become the theme for many films
by Warner Brothers, excluding, of course, the *Looney Tunes* cartoons starring Bugs Bunny. It's time to end this meandering essay,
which has ridiculously gone from Benny to Bunny. So let's put on a
real or mental recording of Gordon Jenkins' "Goodbye" (1936),
Goodman's closing theme, and think good thoughts of the bandleader who brought so much pleasing and stimulating music to
America.

Sing, Sing, Sing

Whether you "Sing, Sing, Sing" or "Sing, Sing, Sing, Sing," the world of music really swings when that excellent 1937 number by Louis Prima (1910-1978) is performed with great zest (as it is normally done). One of the favorites of the Benny Goodman Orchestra, with much emphasis on percussion instruments, the extended composition was one of the pieces featured in the 1956 film *The Benny Goodman Story*. "Sing, Sing, Sing" was also a favorite of the Louis Prima Orchestra, along with "Way Down Yonder in New Orleans" (1922, by Henry Creamer and J. Turner Layton).

Another song by Prima, the little-known "A Sunday Kind of Love" (1946), written with Barbara Belle, Anita Leonard, and Stan Rhodes, was not in the movie, but a big batch of other Goodman numbers were ("Sunday" was a favorite of the Claude Thornhill Orchestra), including several Goodman favorites and various other pieces. Among the numbers not closely associated with Goodman were the following: "Taking a Chance on Love" (1940), words by John Latouche and Ted Fetter, music by Vernon Duke; "Jersey Bounce" (1942), words by Buddy Feyne and Robert B. Wright, music by Bobby Plater, Tiny Bradshaw, Edward Johnson, and Wright; "It's Been So Long" (1936), words and music by Harold Adamson and Walter Donaldson; "I'm Comin', Virginia" (1926), words and music by Will Marion Cook and Donald Heywood; "S-H-I-N-E" (1924), words by Cecil Mack and Lew Brown, music by Ford Dabney; "One O'Clock Jump" (1938), music by Count Basie and Harry James; "China Boy" (1922), words and music by Dick Winfree and Phil Boutelje; "If You Knew Suzie" (1925), words and music by Bud DeSylva and Joseph Meyer; and "I Got It Bad and That Ain't Good" (1941), words by Paul Francis Webster, music by Duke Ellington.

The following numbers in the film were more closely associated with Goodman: "Avalon" (1920), words and music by Al Jolson and Vincent Rose; "Memories of You" (1930), words by Andy Razaf, music by Eubie Blake; "Bugle Call Rag" (1923), words and music by Jack Pettis, Billy Meyers, and Elmer Schoebel; "And the Angels Sing" (1939), words and music by Johnny Mercer and Ziggy Elman; "Goody, Goody" (1936), words and music by Mercer and Matt Malneck; "You Turned the Tables on Me" (1936), words by Sidney D. Mitchell, music by Louis Alter; "Moonglow" (1934), words by Irving Mills and Eddie DeLange, music by Will Hudson; "Lullaby in Rhythm" (1938), words and music by Benny Goodman, Edgar Sampson, Clarence Prift, and Walter Hirsch; and "Stompin' at the Savoy" (1936), words by Razaf, music by Goodman, Sampson, and Chick Webb.

So much interesting music in one movie! Unfortunately, *The Benny Goodman Story* is not a staple of broadcast or even cable television. Only those music lovers, possibly a minority, who are not overly challenged by the fickle technology of a videocassette recorder can avail themselves of the opportunity to view this swing era classic.

BILLY ECKSTINE
(THE BILLY ECKSTINE ORCHESTRA, 1944-1947)

Prisoner of Love

Billy Eckstine (1914-1993), born William Clarence Eckstein in Pittsburgh, Pennsylvania, was best known as a top vocalist, but he also was a bandleader of some consequence. Among the favorite numbers of the Billy Eckstine Orchestra were "Prisoner of Love" (1931) and "A Cottage for Sale" (1930).

"Prisoner," a good song with a striking title, was written by lyricist Leo Robin (1900-) and musician Russ Columbo (1908-1934). Whereas Columbo, a singer, is not known for any other compositions of note, Robin was a moderately important wordsmith. His other collaborations include "Beyond the Blue Horizon" (1930), with composers Richard A. Whiting and W. Franke Harling; "Love Is Just Around the Corner" (1934), with composer Lewis E. Gensler; "June in January" (1934), "Love in Bloom" (1934), and "Thanks for the Memory" (1937), all three with composer Ralph Rainger; and, perhaps best of all, "Diamonds Are a Girl's Best Friend" (1949), with composer Jule Styne, for the hit musical *Gentlemen Prefer Blondes*.

The Eckstine Orchestra revived "Prisoner of Love" in 1946 as one of its more successful hits. (Others also recorded "Prisoner," including Tiny Tim, the falsetto-voiced ukulele-playing entertainer who produced an album with the title *Prisoner of Love*.) About the same time, the Eckstine group also revived "A Cottage for Sale." "Cottage" was written by lyricist Larry Conley and musician Willard Robison. Neither Conley nor Robison are well known, though Robison also wrote the lyrics to "Head Low" (1929), with music by the equally obscure Frank Skinner.

Without a Song

Although he led a good and successful big band, Billy Eckstine perhaps made his biggest contributions to American music as a singer. With clear tones, a deep and resonant voice, and excellent presence during performances, he was a standout vocal star to both blacks and whites. Whether the lead singer with the Billy Eckstine Orchestra or rendering a solo or duet with other groups, Eckstine was, for a number of years, a top talent, particularly in the 1940s and 1950s.

It is a bit amusing, then, that one of the many numbers recorded by Eckstine was "Without a Song." Created in 1929 by lyricists Billy Rose (1899-1966) and Edward Eliscu (1902-) and composer Vincent Youmans (1898-1946), "Without a Song" was one of several pieces on a 1945 recording by the Billy Eckstine Orchestra. On this particular disc, Eckstine not only did the vocalizing but also played the trumpet and valve trombone. Other compositions on this notable album were "Together" (1928), words by Bud DeSylva and Lew Brown, music by Ray Henderson; "Mean to Me" (1929), words and music by Roy Turk and Fred E. Ahlert; and "Don't Blame Me" (1933), words by Dorothy Fields, music by Jimmy McHugh.

When not crooning with his own ensemble, Eckstine made some other very good recordings. For example, in 1957, he recorded three famous ballads by Irving Berlin: were "The Girl That I Marry" (1946), "Easter Parade" (1933) (in a duet with Sarah Vaughan), and "Always" (1925) (also with Vaughan). Just as these three quality songs spanned three decades, Eckstine's quality vocal renditions spanned over three decades in spite of the constant dangers of losing the affections of a fickle American public.

BOB CROSBY
(THE BOB CROSBY ORCHESTRA, 1935-1942)

Day In—Day Out

Not every song created becomes a favorite number of three notable big bands. "Day In—Day Out" (1939), words and music by Johnny Mercer and Rube Bloom, was affiliated with the orchestras of Tommy Dorsey, Artie Shaw, and Bob Crosby (1913-1993). Yet, "Day In" is far from a top classic, though quite successful in its time.

Mercer (1909-1976), from Savannah, Georgia, wrote many fine popular songs, including another hit with Bloom, "Fools Rush In" (1940, words by Mercer, music by Bloom). New York City-born Bloom (1902-1976) also wrote noteworthy songs with other collaborators. Bloom wrote several compositions with lyricist Ted Koehler, who worked with the outstanding composer Harold Arlen to produce the classic "Stormy Weather" (1933), the Benny Goodman hit "Get Happy" (1930), and other pieces. The Bloom-Koehler collaborations include "Don't Worry About Me" (1939), "Out in the Cold Again" (1934), and "Truckin'" (1935). With yet another collaborator, lyricist Harry Ruby, Bloom wrote his, perhaps, best song, certainly his most enduring, "Give Me the Simple Life" (1945), which has been recorded by Frank Sinatra, among others. (Ruby's best-known song is probably "Who's Sorry Now?" [1923], a classic written with colyricist Bert Kalmar and composer Ted Snyder.)

In his earlier years, Bloom created two instrumentals, "Song of the Bayou" (1929) and "Soliloquy" (1927). Bloom had a moderate amount of success with his songs, but not as much as his somewhat better-known associates Koehler and Ruby or his quite famous partner Mercer. The same could be said of bandleader Bob Crosby, who often performed Bloom and Mercer's "Day In—Day Out." Crosby definitely was a successful leader, but not one of the big names in the big band game.

In a Little Gypsy Tea Room

Bob Crosby, born George Robert Crosby in Spokane, Washington, was a singer and one of the more successful bandleaders of his time. Bob did not have a vocal career that even approached the legendary heights achieved by his older brother Harry "Bing" Crosby, but he was certainly good enough to sing with some bands in the 1930s. After he formed the Bob Crosby Orchestra, in some manifestations also called the "Bob Cats," he used an engaging personality and good music to become a popular big band leader and an even more popular radio and television personality in the 1940s and 1950s.

Among the numbers favored by Crosby were the following: Crosby's theme, "Summertime" (1935), lyrics by DuBose Heyward (1885-1940) and Ira Gershwin (1896-1983), music by George Gershwin (1898-1937), from the great folk opera *Porgy and Bess;* "For Dancers Only" (1939) by Sy Oliver; "Where the Blue of the Night Meets the Gold of the Day" (1931), words by Bob's brother Bing and Roy Turk, music by Fred E. Ahlert; "In a Little Gypsy Tea Room" (1935), words by Edgar Leslie, music by Joseph A. Burke; and "What's New?" (1939), words and music by Johnny Burke and Robert Haggart. Joseph Burke (1884-1950) and Johnny Burke (1908-1964), though having chronologically overlapping artistic careers, were not only different in first name but different in their historical contributions. Joseph, a generation older, was a composer specializing in more traditional-style compositions, including "Moon Over Miami" (1935), with lyricist Leslie, and "Carolina Moon" (1928), with lyricist Benny Davis. Somewhat better-known Johnny was primarily a lyricist who frequently wrote for the cinema. Among his top songs were "Pennies from Heaven" (1936), with composer Arthur Johnston; "Imagination" (1940) and Academy Award-winner "Swinging on a Star" (1944), both with composer Jimmy Van Heusen; and "Misty" (1955), with composer Erroll Garner.

Bass player Robert, or Bobby, Haggart, who co-authored "What's New?" with Johnny Burke, helped create two other pieces with interesting titles: "Big Noise from Winnetka" (1940), possibly referring to an Illinois city near the windy city, Chicago, was written by Haggart, Bob Crosby, Ray Baudac, and Gil Rodin. "South Rampart Street Parade" (1940) was written by Haggart, Baudac, and pianist and comedian Steve Allen. So if you are ever in a little gypsy tea room and someone asks "What's new?," you can respond with the previous litany of interesting musical associations (and probably bore the inquirer to death).

BUNNY BERIGAN
(THE BUNNY BERIGAN ORCHESTRA, 1937-1942)

I Can't Get Started

Although he had a short life, Fox Lake, Wisconsin-born Roland Bernard Berigan (1909-1942), more commonly known as "Bunny" Berigan, made a significant impact on the swing era. A trumpet player and leader of the Bunny Berigan Orchestra, Berigan was involved with several hit recordings. With the Tommy Dorsey Orchestra in 1937, his solo section for Irving Berlin's 1928 standard "Marie" was widely admired and imitated.

With the Benny Goodman Orchestra in 1935 and 1936, he contributed to the recorded success of Ferdinand "Jelly Roll" Morton's 1924 "King Porter Stomp" and Irving Caesar and Vincent Youman's 1927 "Sometimes I'm Happy," the theme of the Blue Barron Orchestra. (Caesar and Youman also wrote the theme of the Dick Wickman Orchestra, the 1924 standard "I Want to Be Happy.") Berigan's most notable recording, however, was not of a song by an Irving or a composer with a colorful (or sticky) nickname. With his own ensemble, he had a big hit with "I Can't Get Started (with You)," a 1935 composition by an Ira, that is, the famous Ira Gershwin, and a Duke, that is, the also notable Vernon Duke. (Duke actually was a Dukelsky, born Vladimir Dukelsky in Russia.)

That favorite and theme of Bunny Berigan was not the only collaborative number by lyricist Gershwin (1896-1983) and composer Duke (1903-1969). In 1938, Duke completed the music for the classic "Our Love Is Here to Stay," left uncompleted by the premature death of the great George Gershwin. Coupled with brother Ira's fine words, "Our Love" was introduced in the 1938 film *The Goldwyn Follies*. Despite the lack of any perceived folly (except romantic) in either composition, Ira and Duke's earlier collaboration, "I Can't Get Started," was also in a "follies," the *Ziegfeld Follies* of 1936 to 1937. To add to this semantic confusion, another favorite number of Berigan was "Ebb Tide." The "Ebb Tide" performed by his orchestra obviously was not the famous 1953 song by lyricist Carl Sigman and composer Robert Maxwell, but a much less enduring 1937 song by lyricist Leo Robin and composer Ralph Rainger. With Bunny Berigan, George Gershwin, and Ralph Rainger all involved in this essay, nobody can say we couldn't get started with alliteration.

When Yuba Plays
the Rumba on His Tuba

There is nothing particularly notable, historically or artistically, about "When Yuba Plays the Rumba on His Tuba." It was not a big hit, nor was it a special favorite of a big band. Its most notable feature is its amusing title, which on top of the rhyme of "Yuba" and "tuba," suggests a somewhat ridiculous scene in which a fast-paced rumba is attempted on an instrument designed for slower passages. However, "Yuba" does have one little niche in the story of American music. It was one of the numbers recorded in 1931 by top trumpet player, and later bandleader, Bunny Berigan, then around twenty-two years old.

Also known as "When Yuba Plays the Tuba," the 1931 piece was created by little-known Herman Hupfield or Hupfeld (1894-1951). A better-known song by Hupfield, "As Time Goes By" (1931), was also one of the songs on the Berigan recording, which has as one of its titles *The Essential Young Bunny Berigan*. "As Time" did not become famous until it became a key ingredient in the legendary 1942 Humphrey Bogart and Ingrid Bergman film *Casablanca*.

Among the other numbers on the same recording were "The Hour of Parting" and "Just One More Chance." "The Hour" (1931) was by the successful wordsmith Gus Kahn, who cowrote a number of good songs, and by little-known composer Mischa Spoliansky. "Just One" (1931) was cocreated by two little-known songwriters, Sam Coslow and Arthur Johnston. (Another better-known work, "Pennies from Heaven" [1936], was written by composer Johnston with lyricist Johnny Burke.) With both little-known songs and little-known songwriters being featured in this essay, there is plenty of potential for some philosophical wanderings. However, at this point in this sufficiently lengthy word cluster, it is the hour of parting and the reader should not give the author just one more chance to write any more.

CAB CALLOWAY
(THE CAB CALLOWAY ORCHESTRA, 1930-1948)

Jumpin' Jive

If the reader has no idea as to the general style and mood of the jazz number "Jumpin' Jive" or "Hip Hop the Jumpin' Jive," then a few basic lessons in music may be necessary. Obviously not a placid ballad, lullaby, or reflective sleep-inducer, "Jumpin'," in the language of popular music, literally jumps into artistic action. In 1939, when it was written, it also jumped into the hearts of many Americans. Created by African-American bandleader Cab Calloway (1907-1994) and composer Jack Palmer, "Jumpin'" became a favorite of the Cab Calloway Orchestra.

Palmer wrote several other songs with interesting titles. With Clarke Van Ness he created "Aunt Jemima (Silver Dollar)" (1939), for an Aunt Jemima pancakes advertisement, and "Silver Dollar (Down and Out)" (1950). About half a generation before 1939, Palmer, with Spencer Williams, wrote "Everybody Loves My Baby, but My Baby Don't Love Nobody but Me" (1924). However, in 1925, the duo not only came up with a shorter title but perhaps contradicted the song from the previous year when they came out with "I Found a New Baby."

Williams, a better-known composer than Palmer, wrote two other notable jazz numbers: "Royal Garden Blues" (1919), by Clarence

Williams and Spencer Williams, was recorded successfully by the Tommy Dorsey Orchestra and "Basin Street Blues" (1929), written by Spencer alone, may well approach the status of a jazz classic. The real classic in all of this, however, is Calloway himself, a man of much talent, and even more charm, who made significant contributions to jazz and to American popular culture overall.

Minnie the Moocher

He was nicknamed "the hi-de-ho man" and was nationally known for his "scat" singing, that is, for his substitution of nonsense lyrics for real lyrics while simulating musical instruments; his theme was something called "Minnie the Moocher." While these credentials may not appear to describe a top artist and entertainer, they are among the characteristics that made Cab Calloway one of the most beloved figures in American popular culture.

Born Cabell Calloway in Rochester, New York, he was a most engaging singer and movie actor, as well as a bandleader of note. The song with which he was most associated, both as a vocalist and as a bandleader, was the aforementioned "Minnie the Moocher." Written by Calloway, Irving Mills (1894-1985), and Clarence Gaskill, and recorded by Calloway in 1931, "Minnie" charmingly paraded Calloway's "scat" technique. (The origins of "scat" are uncertain. Is the term based on "scatological," that is, pertaining to excrement, or on "scatter," or on something relating to "cat," which in jazz parlance means a devotee to jazz?) His nickname, "the hi-de-ho man," is based on the usage of such sounds in the song, and, accordingly, variant titles for "Minnie" include "The Hi De Ho Song" and "The Ho De Ho Song." As if this curious little piece were not complicated enough, it was based on the traditional folksong "Willy the Weeper," which also had an alliterative title.

Not all songs affiliated with Calloway and the Cab Calloway Orchestra had such unconventional or unusual traits. Another favorite of Calloway, and a number of other artists, was the outstanding jazz composition "Blues in the Night." Moody "Blues," a marked contrast from light-hearted "Minnie," was written in 1941 by two outstanding songwriters, lyricist Johnny Mercer and musician Harold Arlen. Apparently, Calloway, similar to the rest of us, had mirthful "Minnie" moments as well as sad sessions.

CHARLIE BARNET
(THE CHARLIE BARNET ORCHESTRA, 1933-1944)

Cherokee

Ray (Raymond Stanley) Noble (1903-1978) was a notable band-leader and, in addition, was a notable composer who created a theme for another notable bandleader, Charlie (Charles Daly) Barnet (1913-1991). Introspective, yet appealing, "Cherokee" (1939, words and music by Noble) is one of the better compositions of the swing era and Barnet's biggest hit. Noble, born in Brighton, England, also wrote two other well-known pieces: "The Very Thought of You" (1934, words and music by Noble) and "Goodnight, Sweetheart" (1931, words and music by Noble, James Campbell, and Reginald Connelly). "Very Thought" is a tender love song, and the standard "Goodnight, Sweetheart" is a direct and personal ballad that was in the everyday repertory of crooner Rudy Vallée.

Several other compositions came from the talented pen of Noble, all on the subdued or sentimental side. "Brighter Than the Sun" (1932), "I Hadn't Anyone Till You" (1938), "Love Is the Sweetest Thing" (1933), and "The Touch of Your Lips" (1936) were entirely by Noble. With collaborator Alan Murray he created "I'll Be Good Because of You" (1931), with collaborator Max Kester he wrote "Love Locked Out" (1933, words by Kester, music by Noble), and with collaborators Campbell and Connelly he also wrote "By the Fireside" (1932) and "I Found You" (1931).

His most frequent collaborators, Campbell and Connelly, created another soft-sided song, "Try a Little Tenderness" (1932), with Harry Woods. Despite the semantic implications of the names of Noble, Reginald (royalty), and Campbell (a dominant Scottish clan), their music definitely was intended for enjoyment by the masses, with not the slightest hint of pretense in the good, but approachable, pieces they left behind.

Skyliner

The title "Skyliner" gives the distinct impression of casually and dreamily floating through the atmosphere or the cosmos, with a very pleasurable trip being experienced by all of the fortunate passengers. The content of the theme of the Charlie Barnet Orchestra matches these impressions very well. One of the better big band themes, "Skyliner" (1945, words and music by New York City-born saxophonist Barnet) helped transport Barnet and his ensemble to commercial success.

Other favorite songs for the Barnet ensemble were "Redskin Rhumba" (1941) by Barnet, at one time Barnet's theme; "Cherokee" (1939), words and music by fellow bandmaster Ray Noble; "I Hear a Rhapsody" (1941), words and music by George Frajos, Jack Baker, and Dick Gasparre, which was revived in 1952; and "Where Was I?" (1940), words by Al Dubin, music by W. Franke Harling. The last composition was written for the film *Till We Meet Again*. Its creators, Dubin and Harling, are also known for other works. Lyricist Dubin collaborated on a number of noteworthy pieces, including "Lullaby of Broadway" (1935), with composer Harry Warren, and "Tip Toe Through the Tulips" (1929), with composer Joseph A. Burke. Musician Harling was less accomplished, yet he and Richard A. Whiting cowrote the melody for "Beyond the Blue Horizon" (1930) to accompany the lyrics by Leo Robin. ("Beyond" was the theme of the George Olsen Orchestra.)

"Beyond the Blue Horizon" and "Skyliner" have something in common besides the indirect artistic connection between Barnet and Harling. Both numbers give the listener the same aesthetic sense or psychological feeling of soft and soothing movement in a worry-free or ideal environment. This mellow mood, which can be attained while lying on a couch at home, helps to relieve us of our cares and concerns in a more inexpensive way than lying on a couch in a psychiatrist's office.

CHARLIE SPIVAK
(THE CHARLIE SPIVAK ORCHESTRA, 1940-1947)

Linda

Ann Ronell did not write numerous songs, but among the songs she did create were "Willow Weep for Me" (1932) and "Linda" (1944, co-authored by Jack Lawrence), which includes the memorable line "With one lucky break, I'll make Linda mine." For the Walt Disney animated short *The Three Little Pigs* (1933), Ronell, with Frank E. Churchill, wrote "Who's Afraid of the Big Bad Wolf?". That delightful ditty, with its three sassy renderings of the three-word phrase "big bad wolf" in each verse, derived its melody mostly from "The Champagne Song" section of Johann Strauss Jr.'s 1874 opera *Die Fledermaus*. Coming in the midst of the Great Depression, "Who's Afraid" became a sort of anti-Depression symbol that sassed the specter of the big economic downturn.

Churchill, with Larry Morey, also composed three other enduring, Disney-related songs: "Some Day My Prince Will Come," "Whistle While You Work," and "Heigh Ho." These were written for Disney's first full-length animated movie, *Snow White and the Seven Dwarfs* (1937).

One group animated by the song "Linda" was the Charlie Spivak Orchestra. Spivak (1907-1982), born in Kiev, Ukraine, grew up in the United States and played trumpet with various orchestras before he formed his own. "Linda," a charming and danceable standard, was a favorite of the Spivak Orchestra.

My Devotion

Longevity for any musical group depends on a number of factors, including the choice of music to be performed. The Charlie Spivak Orchestra, for example, chose to play both popular classics and lesser-known pieces. Spivak's ensemble was not the best-known swing band, but it lasted for decades because Spivak knew what the public wished to hear and didn't mind accommodating audiences.

One Spivak favorite that is not particularly famous was "My Devotion." Created in 1942 by obscure songwriters Roc Hillmann and Johnny Napton, it was, however, well enough liked to be not only embraced by a noteworthy big band but also included in a 1943 film, *Follow the Band*. That production also included "He's My Guy" (1942), by better-known songwriters Don Raye and Gene DePaul, and a patriotic classic, "The Air Force Song" (1939), by Robert M. Crawford.

Although Spivak did not record the songs for the 1943 movie, on other occasions, he recorded a similar mix of numbers. In the same year that "My Devotion" appeared, Spivak recorded the World War II favorite "I Left My Heart at the Stage Door Canteen" (1942), written by Irving Berlin for the Broadway musical *This Is the Army*. Some years later, a 1950s collection of several Spivak renditions included a classic, Berlin's "White Christmas" (1942); a fine standard, "Ballerina" or "Dance Ballerina, Dance" (1947, by lyricist Bob Russell and composer Carl Sigman); and two less familiar pieces, "Come Closer to Me" and "We Could Make Such Beautiful Music (Together)." "Come Closer," originally "Acercate Mas," was created in 1946 by Osvaldo Farres. The translation from Spanish was by Al Stewart. "Beautiful Music" (1940, revived in 1947) was by lyricist Robert Sour and musician Henry Manners. However, the overall manner of the Spivak Orchestra was far from sour, and, for years, they made beautiful music together.

CHICK WEBB
(THE CHICK WEBB ORCHESTRA, 1926-1939)

A-Tisket, A-Tasket

If ever there was a queen or princess of the big band era, it was Ella Fitzgerald. Born in Newport News, Virginia, Fitzgerald (1918-1996) has often been described as the best female jazz vocalist, and also as the best female singer in twentieth-century American popular culture. In 1935, young Ella was hired as a vocalist for the Chick Webb Orchestra, helping to propel both the singer and the band toward the top of artistic and commercial success.

Fitzgerald made a number of recordings with Webb (1909-1939), but perhaps none was more important than her charming rendition of a simple, almost naive, number about losing a little yellow basket. "A-Tisket, A-Tasket" (1938), based on an American nursery rhyme that first appeared around 1879, was written by Fitzgerald and Al Feldman. It was a hit in 1938 and in 1944, and film and record excerpts of her bouncily performing the piece have more than occasionally served as examples of her craft.

The success of "A-Tisket, A-Tasket" was promptly followed by another song in which the little yellow basket was found. "I Found My Yellow Basket" (1938) was created by Fitzgerald and Webb. "I Found," however, was not the first composition collaboration by the two. In 1937, Fitzgerald, Webb, Bud Green, and Teddy McCrae produced "You Showed Me the Way." This number was introduced by the Benny Goodman Orchestra, thus providing one more notable artistic nugget for Ella to carry in her little yellow basket.

Stompin' at the Savoy

African-American bandleader Chick Webb was definitely a musician of note during the 1930s. His accomplishments, in addition, were achieved despite neurological problems that had plagued him almost since birth. Born William Webb in Baltimore, Maryland, Webb became a drummer, and by 1931 his band had become a regular at the Savoy Ballroom in New York City. After adding vocalist Ella Fitzgerald to the Chick Webb Orchestra in 1935, the ensemble soared in popularity until Webb's untimely death due to complications from his chronic illnesses and the failure of several spinal operations.

The number most associated with Webb was "Stompin' at the Savoy" (1936), words by the prominent African-American lyricist Andy Razaf (1895-1973), with music by Webb, another notable African-American musician, Edgar Sampson (1907-1973), who was a top arranger, and the great bandleader Benny Goodman (1909-1986). "Stompin'" was also a favorite of the Benny Goodman Orchestra. Another composition by Webb was "You Can't Be Mine (and Someone Else's Too)" (1938, words by Webb and W. C. Johnson, music by Johnson).

Other numbers recorded by Webb include the following, most of which are standards or swing era favorites: "I May Be Wrong, but I Think You're Wonderful" (1929), Webb's theme, words by Harry Ruskin, music by Henry Sullivan; "The Dipsy Doodle" (1937), by Larry Clinton; "Don't Be That Way" (1938), by Goodman, Sampson, and Mitchell Parish; "Hallelujah!" (1927), words by Clifford Grey and Leo Robin, music by Vincent Youmans; "Heebie Jeebies" (1926), by Boyd Atkins; "Little White Lies" (1930), a top favorite of the Tommy Dorsey Orchestra, by Walter Donaldson; "My Heart Belongs to Daddy" (1938), by Cole Porter; "On the Sunny Side of the Street" (1930), words by Dorothy Fields, music by Jimmy McHugh; "Sweet

Sue" (1928), words by Will J. Harris, music by Victor Young; and "Undecided" (1939), a top favorite of the John Kirby Orchestra, words by Sid Robin, music by Charlie Shavers. This partial listing suggests that Webb was adept at recognizing good music and superior artists.

CLAUDE THORNHILL
(THE CLAUDE THORNHILL ORCHESTRA, 1940-1942, 1946-1948, SPORADICALLY THEREAFTER)

Loch Lomond

Somehow it seems incongruous to hear the sentimental and introspective lines, "Oh, ye'll take the high road and I'll take the low road, and I'll be in Scotland afore ye" in the middle of the jazz-oriented swing era. Yet "Loch Lomond," the famous folk piece published in Edinburgh around 1876, was a hit recording in 1937 and was adopted as the theme of the Billy McDonald Orchestra.

A better-known bandleader, Claude Thornhill (1909-1965), was extensively involved with the 1937 version of "Loch Lomond," although he had not yet formed his first band. Thornhill made an arrangement of the lovely old ballad that was used in 1937 recordings by the Benny Goodman Orchestra and the Maxine Sullivan Orchestra. Thornhill also directed Sullivan's ensemble during the recording while Sullivan did the vocalizing. (Sullivan, incidentally, was for a while closely associated with another bandleader, John Kirby, whom she married.) The same Thornhill-Sullivan combination also performed the number on the flip side of the "Loch Lomond" recording, "I'm Comin', Virginia" or "I'm Coming, Virginia" (1926, by Will Marion Cook and Donald Heywood). A 1941 recording of "Loch Lomond" by Sullivan, using Thornhill's arrangement, substituted Seymour Simons and Nora Bayes' "Just Like a Gypsy" (1919) on the flip side.

The Scottish song, in addition to being revived during a period dominated by jazz and dance numbers, also provides fodder for the artistic dichotomies faced by many of the big bands. Some of the ensembles went back and forth between standard pops and jazz, and other ensembles wavered between swing and other jazz forms, such as the blues. So, using the famous lines from the folk song to exemplify these dichotomies, we get:

> Oh, ye'll take the pops road and
> I'll take the jazz road, and
> I'll be in band land afore ye

or

> Oh, ye'll take the swing road and
> I'll take the blues road, and
> I'll be in jazz land afore ye.

Snowfall

"Snowfall" may seem a curious favorite for a big band, but, nevertheless, it was the theme song of the Claude Thornhill Orchestra. Written as a piano composition in 1941 by Thornhill, "Snowfall" was his signature piece. Thornhill, born in Terre Haute, Indiana, was a pianist and arranger as well as a composer and notable bandleader who earned considerable respect from other musicians. To a large extent, this admiration came from the fine texture of tones created by his original band, which included, uncommonly, the use of French horns.

Another favorite number of Thornhill was "A Sunday Kind of Love" (1946), written by Barbara Belle, Anita Leonard, Stan Rhodes, and Louis Prima. The only other notable composition produced by any member of this foursome was "Sing, Sing, Sing," the exuberant Benny Goodman favorite written by Prima in 1937.

On the flip side of Thornhill's 1941 recording of "Snowfall," incidentally, was "Where or When?", a more enduring and more famous song. From the outstanding 1937 Broadway musical by the great team of composer Richard Rodgers and lyricist Lorenz Hart, *Babes in Arms*, "Where or When?" could suggest a perhaps unanswerable question. That is, "Where or when was the last time anybody played 'Snowfall' or 'A Sunday Kind of Love,' the two good but generally overlooked numbers most associated with Claude Thornhill?"

CLYDE McCOY
(THE CLYDE McCOY ORCHESTRA, 1920-1960s, OCCASIONAL TOURS THROUGH EARLY 1980s)

Sugar Blues

The words "sugar" and "blues" may seem to be somewhat contradictory, but the hit number "Sugar Blues" was far from contradictory to the success of the Clyde McCoy Orchestra. Recorded by McCoy in 1931, and rerecorded several times, "Sugar Blues" sold millions of records and became McCoy's theme song.

Created in 1923 by lyricist Lucy Fletcher and musician Clarence Williams (1893-1965), the blues song with the sweet title was only one of several well-known blues compositions associated with persons named Williams. Clarence and unrelated Spencer Williams collaborated on "Royal Garden Blues" (1919), which was recorded by the Tommy Dorsey Orchestra. Spencer (1889-1965) also wrote "Basin Street Blues" (1929), a possible jazz classic, and collaborated with Dave Peyton on the music for another top blues song (but without "blue" in the title), "I Ain't Got Nobody." The last song (1916, lyrics by Roger Graham) became the theme song of African-American bandleader Bert Williams (1877-1922), also unrelated.

Another blues number that was the theme of an orchestra was "Bye, Bye, Blues." Written in 1930 by Fred Hamm, Dave Bennett, Bert Lown, and Chauncey Gray, although based on James H. Rogers' "The Star" (1912), "Bye, Bye" was the signature number of Bert Lown and his Hotel Biltmore Orchestra. Lown and Gray also created the melody for "You're the One I Care For" (1930) to accompany Harry Link's lyrics.

We have touched upon three Williams, two Daves, and two Berts, and now we will mention another Gray. The Clyde McCoy Orchestra also had a hit with "Smoke Rings," the theme of the Glen Gray Orchestra. ("Smoke" was created in 1932 by lyricist Ned Washington and composer H. Eugene Gifford.) But, there was only one Clyde McCoy. Born in Ashland, Kentucky, McCoy (1903-1990) used a mute to develop an unusual or even unique "wah wah" sound on his trumpet. That style was the real Clyde McCoy, as was his often-recorded theme. Although McCoy had a number of other hits, including "Tear It Down" (1934, by McCoy and Edna Whistler), "Blue Prelude" (1933, a theme of Woody Herman, words by Gordon Jenkins, music by Joe Bishop), and "Blue Fantasy" (1938, by Frankie Carle and Raymond Leveen), "Sugar Blues" and McCoy were almost synonymous.

COUNT BASIE
(THE COUNT BASIE ORCHESTRA,
1935-1982)

Blue and Sentimental

The music of Count Basie (1904-1984) could be either blue or sentimental, and in the case of "Blue and Sentimental," it could be both at the same time. One of Basie's favorites, "Blue and Sentimental" (1938) was written by Basie and two other notable songwriters, Mack David and Jerry Livingston. David and Livingston also collaborated on "A Dream Is a Wish Your Heart Makes" (1949) and "Bibbidi, Bobbidi, Boo" (1949), both with Al Hoffman. Among other things, David (1912-) wrote lyrics for two classics. He created English lyrics for "La Vie en Rose" (1946, music by Louiguy) and in 1954, for Max Steiner's "Tara's Theme" from the great 1939 film *Gone with the Wind*. Livingston (1909-) also cowrote the famous novelty number "Mairzy Doats" (1943), with Hoffman and Milton Drake, and the lesser-known ballad "I'd Give a Million Tomorrows" (1939), with the better-known Milton Berle. The latter piece was recorded in 1939 by the also better-known Arthur Godfrey. "Mairzy Doats" was one of the themes of the Al Trace Orchestra, along with "You Call Everybody Darling" (1946), by Sam Martin, Ben L. Trace, Clem Watts, and Albert J. Trace. ("Clem Watts" was a pseudonym of Albert Trace.)

"Blue and Sentimental," on which David, Livingston, and Basie collaborated, was recorded by Basie in 1947. The following are other Basie pieces that are, perhaps, not as well-known: "John's Idea" (1937), by Basie and trombonist and guitarist Eddie Durham; "Every Tub" (1938), words by Jon Hendricks, music by Durham and Basie; "Good Morning Blues" (1938), by Basie, Durham, and vocalist Jimmy Rushing; "Swinging the Blues" (1938), by Basie and Durham; "Baby, Don't Tell on Me" (1939), by Rushing, Basie, and Lester Young; "Don't You Miss Your Baby?" (1939), by Durham, Basie, and Rushing; "Sent for You Yesterday and Here You Come Today" (1939), by Basie; "Goin' to Chicago Blues" (1941), by Rushing and Basie; "King Joe" (1941), words by Richard Wright, music by Basie; "Harvard Blues" (1942), words by Eddie Frazier, music by Basie; "Red Bank Boogie" (1943), by Basie and trumpeter Buck Clayton; "Good Bait" (1944), by Todd Dameron and Basie; "Bill's Mill" (recorded 1947), by Basie and Gene Roland; "Ain't It the Truth" (1945), words by Jack Palmer, music by Basie and Buster Harding; "Sweets" (recorded 1950), by Basie and trumpet player Harry Edison, who adopted the number as a favorite when he formed the Harry Edison Orchestra in the 1950s; "Just a Minute" (recorded 1947), by Basie and trombonist William "Dickie" Wells; "If You See My Baby" (recorded 1950), by Basie, pianist Humphrey "Teddy" Brannon, and a third musician named Sam Theard; "Seventh Avenue Express" (recorded 1947), by Basie and Clayton; "Brand New Wagon" (recorded 1947), by Basie and Rushing; "Bye, Bye, Baby" (recorded 1947), by Basie and Rushing; "Mr. Roberts' Roost" (recorded 1947), by Basie, Harding, and Milton Ebbins; and "Basie's Basement" (recorded 1947) by Basie.

Another famous sentimental song recorded in 1947 by the Count Basie Orchestra was "Shine On, Harvest Moon" (1908), words and music by Jack Norworth and Nora Bayes, which was the theme of the Jimmy Joy Orchestra.

One O'Clock Jump

As suggested by his noble title, William "Count" Basie was a giant in the area of jazz. Born in Red Bank, New Jersey, and taught music by his mother, pianist, composer, and bandleader Basie, for a while based in Kansas City, Missouri, was a notable figure of the 1930s, 1940s, and after. However, as is also suggested by his acquired title, "Count," which in English upper-class circles is two levels below the title of "Duke," Basie is not as accomplished as his superlative contemporary Duke Ellington.

Basie's band was less popular than Ellington's, particularly with the majority white population, and his compositions were, overall, not as successful as Ellington's. Yet he did create some pieces of note, including his theme song, "One O'Clock Jump" (1938), an active instrumental written with fellow bandleader Harry James, and its lesser-known sequel "Two O'Clock Jump" (1941), with James and Benny Goodman. A derivative of "Jump," "One O'Clock Boogie," devised in the mid-1940s by Basie, Jimmy Mundy, and Milton Ebbins, was recorded in 1947. This boogie was just one of a number of artistic efforts to cash in on the boogie-woogie fad during the 1930s and 1940s. Another work created by Basie and Ebbins, along with Ben Jackson, was "Basie Blues," which was recorded in 1953.

Two other good pieces, created by Basie alone, were the theme for the late 1950s television program *M Squad,* and one of his top numbers, "Jumpin' at the Woodside" (1938). Whether it was one o'clock in the morning or any other time or place, Count Basie kept much of America jumping to his jive and jazz for decades.

Open the Door, Richard

After the rock and roll era had started to dominate the popular music scene by the late 1950s, and completely overwhelmed it in the 1960s and 1970s, observers of American culture could look back to see if the new, brash musical phenomenon had any discernible artistic predecessors. One song that might fit that description is "Music, Music, Music," or "Put Another Nickel in, in the Nickelodeon," a 1950 piece by Stephan Weiss and Bernie Baum. As belted out by Teresa Brewer in a hit recording, the volume and heavy beat of this just-before-rock composition could be interpreted as leading up to rock and roll.

The same applies to the 1947 hit "Open the Door, Richard." That gusty and earthy song by lyricists "Dusty" Fletcher and John Mason, with composers Jack McVea and Dan Howell, has the feel of an early rock song, even if the American public at the time did not detect any signs of a shift in the winds of popular music. "Open the Door" was a favorite number of the Count Basie Orchestra, one of several not actually composed by the great Basie. Among the non-Basie numbers played by the Basie ensemble were "Doggin' Around" (1938), by Herschel Evans, and a better-known piece, the delectable and sophisticated ballad "After You've Gone" (1918). The creators of the last song were Henry Creamer and J. Turner Layton, who also came up with the lively and unsophisticated banjo number "Way Down Yonder in New Orleans" (1922).

It is possible that Basie did play "Way Down Yonder" at least once, but since that piece didn't really fit his jazz-oriented style, such a performance would have been rare. In contrast, "After You're Gone," which could be described as a quasi-blues piece, has often been performed by various jazz artists with various styles. A similar thing can be said of another swing era favorite with "gone" in the title, Einar A. Swan's 1931 jewel "When Your Lover Has Gone." Among others, Louis Armstrong has lent his talents to this underrated ballad.

Sugar

The 1920s and 1930s were sweet artistic times for jazz ensembles, even when they had economic or personal troubles. The big bands of the late 1920s and 1930s, often jazz ensembles, performed a lot of sweet music, no matter what the circumstances may have been away from the bandstand. Some of the numbers played by the big bands even had titles reminiscent of tasty sweets.

One of the favorites of the Count Basie Orchestra was "Sugar" (1927), written by Maceo Pinkard and Sidney D. Mitchell. (It would be easy to confuse Pinkard and Mitchell's 1927 "Sugar" with another 1927 "Sugar," by Jack Yellen, Milton Ager, Frank Crum, and Red Nichols. The last collaborator was also a bandleader of note who wrote "Nervous Charlie Stomp" [1926] with George Crozier. The theme of the Red Nichols Orchestra, at one time called Red Nichols and his Five Pennies [although numbering as many as nine], was Harry Warren's mournful 1932 instrumental "Wail of the Winds.") The best-known song by Pinkard, furthermore, actually includes the word "Sweet." In 1925 he, bandleader Ben Bernie, and Kenneth Casey cowrote the jazz classic "Sweet Georgia Brown." Another notable piece by Pinkard, "Gimme a Little Kiss, Will Ya, Huh?" (1926, words by Roy Turk and Jack Smith, music by Pinkard) implies sweetness. Also played by Basie was his own 1940s number, with a title appropriate for this essay, "Sweets." ("Sweets," recorded in 1950, was co-authored by Harry Edison.)

Another "sweet" song associated with a big band was the seemingly contradictory "Sugar Blues" (1923), words by Lucy Fletcher, music by Clarence Williams, which was the theme song of Clyde McCoy. One more sweet-titled big band favorite was "Honeysuckle Rose" (1929), words by Andy Razaf, music by Thomas "Fats" Waller. The same year that Razaf and Waller wrote that piece, they, along with Harry Brooks, also created their classic "Ain't Misbehavin'" (1929). The mention of the latter song doesn't mean the chain of sweetness has been broken, for "Ain't Misbehavin'" was written for the revue *Hot Chocolates*.

So, for Count Basie, Clyde McCoy, and other big bands, you didn't have to be labeled "sweet band" to play these sugar-flavored compositions or others, such as "Sweet Sue" (1928), by lyricist Will J. Harris and composer Victor Young. Let's end here, so that we can be both short and sweet.

THE DORSEY BROTHERS (THE DORSEY BROTHERS ORCHESTRA, 1932-1935)

Chasing Shadows

Two lesser-known American popular artists were lyricist Benny Davis (1895-1979) and composer Abner Silver. Although they chased fame, as did most other composers, they were only shadows in the bright light of a number of other more famous contemporary songwriters. It is, therefore, a bit ironic that perhaps their best-known joint composition was the 1935 Dorsey Brothers favorite "Chasing Shadows." Despite the affiliation of that piece with the Dorseys, that number and three others by them, "There Goes My Heart" (1934), "With These Hands" (1950), and "Angel Child" (1922, with George Price), did not bring them any real degree of fame.

When teamed with other collaborators, however, Davis, born in New York City, made a noticeable mark on the history of American music. With composers Con Conrad and J. Russel Robinson, lyricist Davis wrote the standard "Margie" (1920); with composer Harry Akst, Davis wrote the near-classic "Baby Face" (1926); and with composer Joseph A. Burke, Davis wrote the standard "Carolina Moon" (1928).

Another favorite Dorsey Brothers number, "Lullaby of Broadway," was much more popular than Davis and Silver's "Chasing Shadows." "Lullaby," created by two of the contemporary composers that helped cover Davis with the shadows of obscurity, was written by lyricist Al Dubin (1891-1945) and composer Harry Warren (1893-1981) for the 1935 film musical *Gold Diggers of 1935*. Dubin and Warren as a team also wrote "You're Getting to Be a Habit with Me" (1932), "Shuffle Off to Buffalo" (1932), "We're in the Money" (1933), "I Only Have Eyes for You" (1934), and "Lulu's Back in Town" (1935). "Lullaby" won an Academy award for Dubin and Warren, an accomplishment duplicated by Warren with the great lyricist Johnny Mercer for "On the Atchinson, Topeka, and the Santa Fe," which appeared in the 1946 film *The Harvey Girls*. "Lullaby" also has a tongue-in-cheek title and clever lyrics, for anyone who has ever been on Broadway in New York City knows that it is very difficult to sleep in that ever-hustling, ever-bustling twenty-four-hour environment of activity.

Lost in a Fog

The Dorsey brothers, of Shenandoah, Pennsylvania, both together and separately, were immortals of the swing era. Despite their parting of ways in 1935, Tommy and Jimmy were honored together in the 1947 movie *The Fabulous Dorseys.*

The Dorsey numbers played in the film included "Marie" (1928) and "Everybody's Doin' It" (1911), both by Irving Berlin; "Green Eyes" (1929), original Spanish lyrics ("Aquellos ojos verdes") by Adolfo Utrera, English lyrics by L. Wolfe Gilbert, music by Nilo Menendez; "At Sundown" (1927), words and music by Walter Donaldson; and the delightful winner "The Object of My Affection" (1934), words and music by Pinky Tomlin, Coy Poe, and Jimmie Grier.

With so many fine songs played live and in recording studios, the Dorseys lived in the bright light of public approval for over two decades. So it seems a bit odd that one of the favorite pieces of the Dorsey Brothers Orchestra was "Lost in a Fog." That 1934 composition was by lyricist Dorothy Fields (1905-1974) and composer Jimmy McHugh (1894-1969), longtime collaborators. Other songs by Fields and McHugh include the standards "I Can't Give You Anything but Love, Baby" (1928), "On the Sunny Side of the Street" (1930), and "I'm in the Mood for Love" (1935). Fields also wrote "The Way You Look Tonight" (1936) and "A Fine Romance" (1936), both with renowned composer Jerome Kern. The last number was made into a fine recording by Louis Armstrong and Ella Fitzgerald.

Another top Dorsey Brothers number was, ironically, "Chasing Shadows" (1935), words and music by Abner Silver and Benny Davis. Although there were definite personal differences between the two Dorseys, leading to their becoming leaders of two distinct ensembles, neither of these excellent musicians could be described as being lost in a fog or as resorting to chasing shadows.

When I Take My Sugar to Tea

The very comedic Marx Brothers were in show business for years, doing their usual monkey business in several hit movies and other venues. One of their more famous films actually paid tribute to their perpetual shenanigans through its title, *Monkey Business*. The 1931 production of the film included two songs: "You Brought a New Kind of Love to Me" (1930) and "When I Take My Sugar to Tea" (1931). The second piece was a Dorsey Brothers favorite, recorded in 1931 with the Boswell Sisters.

The creators of both numbers were Sammy Fain, Irving Kahal, and Pierre Norman. Fain (1908-1989) and Kahal, without Norman, also collaborated on several other noteworthy songs, including "Let a Smile Be Your Umbrella" (1927), "Wedding Bells Are Breaking Up That Old Gang of Mine" (1929), "I Can Dream, Can't I?" (1937), and "I'll Be Seeing You" (1938). The last composition was recorded in 1944 by Frank Sinatra with the Tommy Dorsey Orchestra, and that rendition was one of the finest and most enduring in Sinatra's long and storied career.

From 1940 to 1942, Sinatra had been a featured vocalist with the Tommy Dorsey Orchestra, but he left to perform on his own. About five years before Sinatra joined the Dorsey ensemble, Tommy the trombonist had disagreements with Jimmy the saxophonist, and the Dorsey Brothers Orchestra split into two groups. That is to say, prior to Sinatra's arrival on the scene, there was a real-life "I'll Be Seeing You."

DUKE ELLINGTON
(THE DUKE ELLINGTON
ORCHESTRA, 1923-1974)

Don't Get Around Much Anymore

The great Duke Ellington (1899-1974) and his outstanding orchestra got around a lot during the many years of their artistic success. It is, therefore, a bit ironic that one of the trademark numbers of Ellington was "Don't Get Around Much Anymore." A favorite on the vaudeville and night club circuits, "Don't Get Around Much Anymore" was written in 1942 by lyricist Bob Russell and composer Ellington, with the melody based on Ellington's "Never No Lament."

Passaic, New Jersey-born Russell (1914-1970), also known as Sidney Keith Russell, collaborated with Ellington on two other notable pieces: "Do Nothin' Till You Hear from Me" (1943), words by Russell, music by Ellington based on his "Concerto for Cootie," and "I Didn't Know About You" (1944), words by Russell, music based on Ellington's "Sentimental Lady." Songs with other collaborators include the following: "East St. Louis Toodle-O" (1927), with B. Miley, a one-time Ellington theme; "I Got It Bad and That Ain't Good" (1941), with lyricist Paul Francis Webster; and the standard "I'm Beginning to See the Light" (1945), with Don George, the famous bandleader Harry James, and Johnny Hodges, a saxophonist in Ellington's orchestra. Hodges later had his own

Johnny Hodges Orchestra, for which "I'm Beginning to See the Light" was a favorite number.

Similar to "Don't Get Around Much," the last two songs are on the ironic side. Ellington had begun to see the light of jazz genius long before 1945, and a summary of his sparkling career might be described by the statement, "I got it good [talent], and that ain't bad!"

It Don't Mean a Thing
If It Ain't Got That Swing

"Irving" and "Mills" are famous names in American music. Irving Berlin was probably the most accomplished American popular composer, and the Mills Brothers were probably the most beloved male vocal group prior to the rock era. But when you put the two names together, forming "Irving Mills," you get much less public appreciation, although there was a lyricist and composer of notable accomplishment with that name.

Irving Mills (1894-1985), born in New York City, was a longtime associate of Duke Ellington who helped create some of Ellington's best pieces. The following numbers were among the Ellington-Mills collaborations: the standard "Sophisticated Lady" (1933), words by Mitchell Parish and Mills, music by Ellington; another standard, "Mood Indigo" (1931), by Mills, Ellington, and Albany Bigard; the excellent "Caravan" (1937), words by Mills, music by Ellington and Juan Tizol (Mills's words for this song, however, are not often heard); "I Let a Song Go Out of My Heart" (1938), words by Mills, Henry Nemo, and John Redmond, music by Ellington; "In a Sentimental Mood" (1935), words and music by Mills, Ellington, and Manny Kurtz (also known as Mann Curtis); "Prelude to a Kiss" (1938), words and music by Mills, Ellington, and Irving Gordon; "Ring Them Bells" (1930), words and music by Mills and Ellington; "Rockin' in Rhythm" (1930), words and music by Mills, Ellington, and Harry Carney; a one-time Ellington theme, "Solitude" (1934), words by Mills and Eddie DeLange, music by Ellington (Mills and DeLange also collaborated on the enduring standard "Moonglow" [1934], with Will Hudson); and the delightful jazz jewel, "It Don't Mean a Thing If It Ain't Got That Swing" (1932), words by Mills, music by Ellington.

Though the music for "It Don't Mean a Thing" is certainly catchy, the lyrics really make this song stand out. Mills has essentially captured the mood of jazz, which is strongly dependent on rhythm, by saying, in effect, "In the jazz world, a tune means nothing if it doesn't have a compelling beat." This insightful bit of pop culture wisdom can also be extended to much of life in general. In any activity that involves bold taste, gusto, energy, and liveliness, such as eating, drinking, sports, or the performing arts, the derived saying "It don't mean a thing if it ain't got that zing" could apply. It can even be appropriate to a romantic relationship. In that case, the line would read, "It don't mean a thing if it ain't got that ring."

Satin Doll

The delicate strains of "Satin Doll" were appropriately named, as is evidenced by the fine musical workmanship of this composition. The last outstanding song by Edward Kennedy "Duke" Ellington, written with cocomposer Billy Strayhorn and lyricist Johnny Mercer, "Satin Doll" was sort of a closing tribute to the greatest of African-American jazz composers.

Ellington, born in Washington, DC, created a impressive list of pieces, with and without words, with and without collaborators. Among the pieces he created without any known assistance were "Black and Tan Fantasy" (1927); "C-Jam Blues" (1942), "Cottontail" (1944); "Creole Love Call" (1932); "Stompy Jones" (1936); and "Diminuendo and Crescendo in Blue" (1937).

The last piece, an extended medium-tempo composition more than fourteen minutes in length, is more esoteric or cerebral than much of his other music and, therefore, perhaps more vulnerable to variations in appreciation. Even the title, with the technical terms "diminuendo" (decreasing in force or volume) and "crescendo" (increasing in force or volume), suggests complexity and mood changes. "Diminuendo" was the climax of Ellington's very successful appearance at the 1956 jazz festival in Newport, Rhode Island.

With the creation of "Satin Doll" two years after the 1956 Newport festival, the 1950s proved a most satisfying period for both Ellington and his adoring audiences. The performance of "Diminuendo" and the composition of "Satin Doll" so near each other shows the versatility of Ellington the classy bandleader and Ellington the talented composer.

Take the "A" Train

Anyone who has taken the subways in New York City to much extent understands what is meant by the "A Train." It is the express service that moves you to your destination a lot faster than the local service that stops at every station.

Dayton, Ohio-born pianist William Thomas Strayhorn (1915-1967), also known as "Sweet Pea," but most commonly known as Billy Strayhorn, was a close, longtime associate of Duke Ellington. In his 1941 classic "Take the 'A' Train," Strayhorn captured the urbaneness and bustle of the big city. Although Ellington had a number of his own compositions from which to choose his theme song, he decided on "'A' Train" to represent his renowned orchestra. In part, this may have been done because "'A' Train" is such a fine piece whether played in a faster, more nervous tempo, as was done by Ellington, or in a more relaxed tempo, as was done by Glenn Miller, or this may also have been done because Ellington and Strayhorn were extremely compatible artistically. Some historians, in fact, believe that Strayhorn may actually have written some works attributed to Ellington.

Strayhorn's "'A' Train" had no lyrics at first, but in 1952, vocalist (and also quite possibly the lyricist) Betty Roche recorded the composition with words attached. Two other notable songs by Strayhorn were the smooth and perhaps classic "Satin Doll" (1958), words by Johnny Mercer, music by Strayhorn and Ellington, and the unusual, yet interesting, "Lush Life" (1938), written totally by himself. The latter piece was recorded in 1949 by the lush vocal chords of the great Nat King Cole, who may have taken the "A Train" at some time in his fabulous career.

ERSKINE HAWKINS
(THE ERSKINE HAWKINS
ORCHESTRA, 1936-LATE 1940s)

Tuxedo Junction

There is more than one way to look at a song. For example, one could note that the swing era standard "Tuxedo Junction" is the number most closely associated with African-American bandleader and trumpeter Erskine Hawkins (1914-1993) and the theme of the Erskine Hawkins Orchestra. One could also note that "Tuxedo" was one of the more famous recordings of the Glenn Miller Orchestra. In addition, one could point out that no less than four artists were apparently needed to create this piece. Lyricist Buddy Feyne and musicians Hawkins, William Johnson, and Julian Dash collaborated on "Tuxedo" in 1940. Johnson and Dash were both saxophonists with the Hawkins ensemble, as was Robert Smith, who wrote "Tippin' In" (recorded 1945), a favorite of the orchestra. A pianist with Hawkins, Avery Parrish, wrote another Hawkins favorite, "After Hours" (recorded 1940).

Although there is a fair amount of history directly connected with "Tuxedo," as previously outlined, approaching the work from a somewhat different angle produces considerably more historical tidbits. If one looks at the quartet that created "Tuxedo," one would discover only one other notable song from any of them. Lyricist Feyne, along with Robert B. Wright, in 1946, supplied lyrics for an earlier hit, "Jersey Bounce." The music for "Jersey" had been composed in 1942 by Wright, Bobby Plater, Tiny Bradshaw, and Edward Johnson. (Note that this second song had five creators, including a different Johnson.) The added words made "Jersey" successful again in 1946, and ten years later, it was one of the songs included in the 1956 film *The Benny Goodman Story.*

Incidentally, Robert B. Wright should not be confused with the better-known songwriter Robert C. Wright, who, with George "Chet" Forrest, collaborated on the hit 1944 musical *Song of Norway,* using the music of Norwegian Edvard Grieg, and on the outstanding 1953 musical *Kismet,* using the music of Russian Alexander Borodin. (This is a lot of additional fascinating information triggered by just one middle initial.)

FRANKIE CARLE
(THE FRANKIE CARLE ORCHESTRA,
1944-LATE 1950s, EARLY 1960s

Oh What It Seemed to Be

Francisco Nunzio Carlone (1903-), born in Providence, Rhode Island, and more commonly known as Frankie Carle, was a bandleader of note and a composer of consequence. Among his compositions were the theme song of the Frankie Carle Orchestra, "Oh What It Seemed to Be" (1946), written with Bennie Benjamin and George David Weiss, and little-known "Blue Fantasy" (1938), written with Raymond Leveen. In addition, seventeen years after Clarence "Pine Top" Smith's "Boogie Woogie" took the world of popular music by storm, Carle wrote his own "Carle Boogie" (1945).

Also, ten years before the French song "Les Feuilles Mortes" ("Autumn Leaves") was written in 1950, Carle somewhat anticipated the concept with his own "Falling Leaves" (1940), put together with Mack David. The more famous French composition was by lyricist Jacques Prévert and composer Joseph Kosma, with English lyrics falling from the competent pen of American wordsmith Johnny Mercer in 1955.

Carle's best-known composition is perhaps "Sunrise Serenade," his one-time theme, written in 1939 with the help of lyricist Jack Lawrence. A favorite number of the Glenn Miller Orchestra, written at a time when Miller's considerable fortunes were rising, "Sunrise" is still often included in retrospective homages to Miller and the big bands. In such glances back to "what it seemed to be," however, Carle is seldom recognized, except for his melody for this fine song.

Rumors Are Flying

Rumors had been flying for thousands of years before Bennie Benjamin and George David Weiss created "Rumors Are Flying" in 1946. In addition to writing this favorite of the Frankie Carle Orchestra, Benjamin and Weiss (1921-) also collaborated on some other pieces of note, including "Wheel of Fortune" (1952), "Cross Over the Bridge" (1954), and "How Important Can It Be?" (1955).

Weiss, away from Benjamin, wrote several hits, such as the following: "Lullaby of Birdland" (1952), with George Shearing; "Wimoweh" or "The Lion Sleeps Tonight" (1952), with Hugo Peretti, Luigi Creatore, and Albert Stanton; "Mr. Wonderful," "Without You I'm Nothing," and "Too Close for Comfort," with Jerry Bock and Larry Holofcener, for the top 1956 musical *Mr. Wonderful;* "Mandolins in the Moonlight" (1958), with Aaron Schroeder; "Can't Help Falling in Love" (1961), with Peretti and Creatore; and "What a Wonderful World" (1968), with George Douglas. Note that Weiss helped create big hits for three top stars, Sammy Davis Jr. ("Mr. Wonderful"), Elvis Presley ("Can't Help"), and Louis Armstrong ("Wonderful World").

On his part, Benjamin helped the career of another bandleader, Vaughn Monroe, when Benjamin, Edward Seiler, and Sol Marcus wrote "When the Lights Go On Again (All Over the World)." The Vaughn Monroe Orchestra, with vocals by Monroe, recorded this World War II era hit, based on Beethoven's "Minuet in G," in 1942. Another top favorite of Monroe was "There! I've Said It Again" (1941), by Redd Evans and Dave Mann, which is occasionally resurrected. Monroe's actual theme song, the dramatic "Racing with the Moon," was created in 1941 by Monroe, Pauline Pope, and Johnny Watson. Also known as John G. Watson, songwriter Watson collaborated with Muriel Watson on a lesser-known piece, "Goodnight to You All" (1937).

GENE KRUPA
(THE GENE KRUPA ORCHESTRA,
1938-1943, 1944-1951)

Boogie Blues

Gene Krupa (1909-1973) was born in Chicago, as was bandleader Benny Goodman, with whom Krupa and his drums were a big attraction in the mid-1930s. Krupa was featured on Goodman's fabulous recording of Louis Prima's "Sing, Sing, Sing" (1937). Krupa was so popular as an energetic drummer that he would have been very famous in the history of jazz even if he were not the leader of one of the more notable big bands. Similar to his associate Goodman, he was honored by a 1959 film, *The Gene Krupa Story,* for which Krupa recorded the sound track with his usual virtuosity.

Part of the Gene Krupa Orchestra's success, of course, was due to the magnetism of Krupa's reputation. Yet his band was popular mainly because of its intrinsic artistry and partly because it selected good music to perform. Krupa had some tendency to prefer numbers not commonly utilized by other groups. Among such pieces were "Apurksody" (1939), by Krupa and Slim Willet, one of Krupa's themes; "Starburst" (1946), by Krupa and Eddie Finckel, another Krupa theme; "Jungle Madness" (1939), by Willet; "It All Comes Back to Me Now" (1941), by Alex C. Kramer, Joan Whitney, and Hy Zaret; "Flamingo" (1941), words by Edmund Anderson, music by Ted Grouya; and "Boogie Blues" (1946), by Krupa and Ray Biondi, a guitarist with Krupa's ensemble. The last song, which sported a title claiming affiliation with two of the more popular, yet quite dissimilar, jazz modes, was recorded by Krupa in 1946.

In addition to his strong direct connection with Goodman, Krupa had an indirect or roundabout tie to another prominent bandleader, Will Bradley. One of Bradley's favorite numbers was "High on a Windy Hill" (1941), by Alex Kramer and Joan Whitney, the song-writing duo who, as you may recall from a few sentences back, wrote the Krupa favorite "It All Comes Back to Me Now" with Hy Zaret.

Let Me Off Uptown

When Redd Evans (1912-1972) and Earl Bostic (1913-1965) created "Let Me Off Uptown" (1941), a fox-trot recorded by the Gene Krupa Orchestra in 1941, they were, in one sense, reflecting the transportation theme of another 1941 composition, Billy Strayhorn's classic "Take the 'A' Train." However, there probably was no direct connection, except coincidence, between the good number adopted by Gene Krupa and the great Strayhorn number adopted by Duke Ellington.

Perhaps the only link between the two 1941 pieces was that both may well have been describing a trip on the strong wind of early 1940s jazz. Evans and Bostic's contribution did not travel nearly as far into the land of public acceptance as did Strayhorn's still-moving orchestral vehicle, but it was on track in 1945 when a new arrangement was made by Bob Morse.

Other songs by Evans, such as the following had some lasting power: "He's 1-A in the Army (and A-1 in My Heart)" (1941), which was popular for much of World War II; "No Moon at All" (1948), words by Evans, music by Dave Mann, which had a surge of popularity in 1952; and "There! I've Said It Again" (1941), by Evans and Mann, which had surges of popularity in 1945, 1947, and 1954. However, nothing by Evans, including "American Beauty Rose" (1950, by Hal David, Arthur Altman, and Evans), and "Don't Go to Strangers" (1954, words by Evans, music by Arthur Kent), had enough artistic fuel to go very far into the future.

GLEN GRAY
(THE CASA LOMA ORCHESTRA AND THE GLEN GRAY ORCHESTRA, 1929-1946)

Blue Moon

So-called "blue moons"—second appearances of the full moon within a calendar month—are rare occurrences. Thus, the expression "once in a blue moon" describes infrequent occasions. Also rare are outstanding songwriting teams. Lorenz Hart (1895-1943) and Richard Rodgers (1902-1979) were partners in one of the best and most enduring of such collaborations, lasting almost a quarter century (twenty-three years) and producing many fine songs and a number of exceptional musicals.

One of the better compositions by wordsmith Hart and master melodist Rodgers was "Blue Moon" (1934). Originally written for the 1934 film *Manhattan Melodrama,* with different lyrics, "The Bad in Every Man," "Blue Moon," a second and much more successful manifestation, was issued independent of the movie. A third manifestation of the moody and enduring ballad was a favorite number of the Glen Gray Orchestra.

Given the rarity of blue moons and the nighttime occurrence of such phenomena, it is perhaps a bit curious that another favorite of Glen Gray was "Sunrise Serenade," which relates to an event occurring every morning, year in and year out. "Sunrise" (1939) was created by lyricist Jack Lawrence and composer Frankie Carle, another bandleader. Also a top number of the Frankie Carle Orchestra, and of yet another ensemble, the Glenn Miller Orchestra, just the one "Sunrise" helped to prolong the days of a trio of big bands.

The days of Lorenz Hart, however, were definitely numbered when his collaboration with Rodgers ended, by Hart's decision, in 1942. The next year, the great musical *Oklahoma* (1943) premiered, cocreated by Rodgers and another exceptional, established professional, lyricist Oscar Hammerstein II. In reaction to this success, talented, but neurotic, Hart went on an alcoholic binge, resulting in his death by pneumonia not long after the new show's debut. The depth of the sad lyrics of "Blue Moon" finally came home to its lyricist.

Smoke Rings

The personal name "Glen" can have one or two "n"s. The famous bandleader Glenn Miller had two "n"s in his first name, and lesser-known, but noteworthy, bandleader Glen Gray had one. Gray (1906-1963), also known as "Spike" Gray, was born Glen Gray Knoblaugh in Roanoke, Illinois. In addition to being an alto sax player, he led the Glen Gray Orchestra, originally the Casa Loma Orchestra, through years of significant success, recording hits as diverse as the sentimental waltz "When I Grow Too Old to Dream" (1935), by lyricist Oscar Hammerstein II and composer Sigmund Romberg, and the jazz standard "Sophisticated Lady" (1933), by lyricists Mitchell Parish and Irving Mills and composer Duke Ellington. The number that most symbolized the artistry of the primarily jazz-oriented ensemble, however, was its theme "Smoke Rings."

Written in 1932 by lyricist Ned Washington and composer H. Eugene "Gene" Gifford, who was an arranger with Gray, "Smoke Rings," although not a classic, has an indirect connection to a big-name big band classic. Wordsmith Washington (1901-1976), one of the better lyricists of his generation, also collaborated on the Tommy Dorsey theme "I'm Getting Sentimental Over You" (1933). Another common ground for both songs was the obscurity of the composers. Neither George Bassman, who created the melody for "I'm Getting Sentimental," nor Gifford (1908-1970), the musician for "Smoke Rings," is known for much else. Gifford, however, did write a jazz piano work worth noting, "Casa Loma Stomp" (1933).

Another indirect connection between Glen Gray and Glenn Miller, in addition to their almost sharing first names, is another bandleader named Gray. Composer and arranger Jerry Gray (1915-1976), born Generoso Graziano in Boston, helped lead the Glenn Miller Orchestra after Miller's untimely death in 1944. Jerry also helped to write some songs of consequence, including two standards of Miller's repertory. He created the melody for one of the top Miller hits, "A String of Pearls" (1942), with lyricist Eddie De-Lange, and the music for another Miller favorite, "Pennsylvania 6-5000" (1939), with lyricist Carl Sigman.

Although literal smoke rings do not have enough physical substance to connect to anything, Glen Gray and his theme have several artistic connections, all of them solid.

GLENN MILLER
(THE GLENN MILLER
ORCHESTRA, 1937-1942,
ARMY AIR FORCE BAND, 1942-1944)

Chattanooga Choo Choo

One of the more memorable and danceable numbers in the repertory of the Glenn Miller Orchestra was "Chattanooga Choo Choo." Written in 1941 by lyricist Mack Gordon (1904-1959) and composer Harry Warren (1893-1981), "Chattanooga" was the best known of several hits by Gordon and Warren that were performed by Miller (1904-1944). The others include the charming "I've Got a Gal in Kalamazoo" (1942), the very much underappreciated "Serenade in Blue" (1942), and the well-crafted "You'll Never Know" (1943).

Warren also cowrote a batch of other pieces available to the big bands. With lyricist Al Dubin, he created "You're Getting to Be a Habit with Me" (1932), "Shuffle Off to Buffalo" (1932), "We're in the Money" (1933), "I Only Have Eyes for You" (1934), "Lulu's Back in Town" (1935), and "Lullaby of Broadway" (1935). With lyricists Mort Dixon and Billy Rose, he wrote "I Found a Million-Dollar Baby" (1931), and with lyricists Dixon and Joe Young, he wrote "You're My Everything" (1931). With lyricist Johnny Mercer, he wrote "Jeepers Creepers" (1938), "You Must Have Been a Beautiful Baby" (1938), and "On the Atchison, Topeka and the Santa Fe" (1945).

The last song, written after Miller's tragic death in an airplane accident on a flight from England to France in December 1944—and therefore not to be material for the original Miller orchestra—is especially interesting in at least two ways. First, it won an Academy Award because of its brilliant simulation of an old-fashioned steam locomotive in the 1946 film *The Harvey Girls* and because of its equally brilliant rendition by the film's female lead, Judy Garland. Second, it is part of an almost perfectly matched pair of railroad songs, with Warren's earlier classic "Chattanooga Choo Choo." With different lyricists, Warren artistically honored Chattanooga, Tennessee, in one composition, Kansas and New Mexico in another, and the romantic traditions of the American railroad in both.

In the Mood

During the heyday of the Glenn Miller Orchestra, from 1939 to late 1944, adoring audiences were definitely in the mood for the music of, perhaps, the most appreciated of the big bands. The classic number "In the Mood" was written in 1939 by lyricist Andy Razaf (1895-1973) and composer Joe Garland. With its relentlessly lively rhythms and coy, playful ending, "Mood" was one of the main reasons for Miller's success. Perhaps the best composition of the swing era, "In the Mood," almost always in the instrumental version, remains a strong favorite today.

"In the Mood" and "Moonlight Serenade" (1939, words by Mitchell Parish, music by Glenn Miller) are the most enduring of the songs recorded by Miller, but a number of other hits written in the 1939 to 1944 period still are revived at least occasionally. These include the following: the World War II classic "Don't Sit Under the Apple Tree" (1939), words by Lew Brown and Charles Tobias, music by Sam H. Stept; the playful "Elmer's Tune" (1941), words and music by Elmer Albrecht, Sammy Gallop, and Dick Jurgens; the excellent standard "A String of Pearls" (1942), words by Eddie DeLange, music by Jerry Gray; the memorable "Pennsylvania 6-5000 (1939), words by Carl Sigman, music by Gray; the dreamy "The Lamplighter's Serenade" (1942), words by Paul Francis Webster, music by Hoagy Carmichael; the more or less forgotten jewel "Moonlight Cocktail" (1942), words by Kim Gannon, music by C. Luckeyth Roberts; the minor hit "Along the Santa Fe Trail" (1940), words by Al Dubin, music by Will Grosz and Edwina Coolidge; the fine, but now mostly overlooked, "Sunrise Serenade" (1939), words by Jack Lawrence, music by Frankie Carle; top hit of the era "Tuxedo Junction" (1940), words by Buddy Feyne, music by Erskine Hawkins, William Johnson, and Julian Dash; and the novelty "Juke Box Saturday Night" (1942), words by Al Stillman, music by Paul McGrane.

"Juke Box," though not especially enduring, is notable because of its effective imitations of Harry James and the Ink Spots, famous contemporary artists. Another notable Miller recording was "Stairway to the Stars" (1935), words by Mitchell Parish, music by Matt Malneck and Frank Signorelli, adapted from "Park Avenue Fantasy." "Stairway" was not one of the songs most closely associated with Miller, but it has been, over the years, closely associated with lovers. Although it is certainly not a great piece, it has often been "the song" for romantic couples who perhaps fantasize about living in wealthy bliss on Park Avenue in New York City.

Little Brown Jug

Although other bandleaders of the swing era also utilized songs from early times in their repertories, Glenn Miller was especially notable for his links to the musical past. Among the well-known pieces of the previous generation that he recorded were "Moonlight Bay" (1912), words by Edward Madden, music by Percy Wenrich; "Peg o' My Heart" (1913), words by Alfred Bryan, music by Fred Fisher, "Who's Sorry Now?" (1923), words by Bert Kalmar and Harry Ruby, music by Ted Snyder; "Johnson Rag" (1917), music by Guy Hall and Henry Kleinauf, words added in 1940 by Jack Lawrence; and "St. Louis Blues March," an adaptation of W. C. Handy's 1914 classic by Jerry Gray.

Going back about two or three generations, Miller recorded "American Patrol" (1885), music by Frank W. Meacham; "Little Brown Jug" (1869), words and music by Joseph Eastburn Winner (1837-1918); and "Song of the Volga Boatmen" (Russian folk song first published in 1866). Going back even further, about four generations, Miller used "The Anvil Chorus" (1853), by Giuseppe Verdi, from his opera *Il Trouvatore,* and "Don't Sit Under the Apple Tree," words written in 1939 by Lew Brown and Charles Tobias, music adapted in 1939 by Sam H. Stept, from Englishman Thomas Haynes Bayly's 1835 composition "Long, Long Ago." Note that all of these, in one manifestation or another, were classics or very famous.

Of the songs derived from the nineteenth century, perhaps none was more enjoyed by Miller's orchestra and contemporary audiences than "Little Brown Jug." That enduring tribute to mirth, merriment, and moonshine was typical of Miller's lighthearted approach to his music. His sense of humor (and of music) was obvious in that number, as in so many others associated with Miller.

Moonlight Serenade

The Glenn Miller Story (1954) was a charming, although somewhat inaccurate, film starring famous actor Jimmy Stewart as the beloved deceased bandleader and notable actress June Allyson as Miller's wife. One of the most appealing aspects of the movie was the brilliant score by Henri Mancini (1924-1994), who later was to become an outstanding popular composer. Mancini wove a number of songs made famous by Miller into a fine swing tapestry, using the Glenn Miller Orchestra supplemented with performances by Louis Armstrong, Gene Krupa, and Joe Yuki (who was the ghost trombonist for Stewart).

The score included the following numbers: "At Last" (1935), words by Charles Tobias and Sam Lewis, music by Henry Tobias; "American Patrol" (1885), music by Frank W. Meacham; "Basin Street Blues" (1929), words and music by Spencer Williams; "Bidin' My Time" (1930), words by Ira Gershwin, music by George Gershwin; "Chattanooga Choo Choo" (1941), words by Mack Gordon, music by Harry Warren, "In the Mood" (1939), words by Andy Razaf, music by Joe Garland; "Moonlight Serenade" (1939), words by Mitchell Parish, music by Miller; "Pennsylvania 6-5000" (1939), words by Carl Sigman, music by Jerry Gray; "A String of Pearls" (1942), words by Eddie DeLange, music by Gray; "Tuxedo Junction" (1940), words by Buddy Feyne, music by Erskine Hawkins, William Johnson, and Julian Dash; and "I Know Why" (1941), words by Gordon, music by Warren.

"Moonlight Serenade" was the signature song of the Miller Orchestra, as well as the only composition of Miller, who was born in Clarinda, Iowa. It was also the theme of the Tex Beneke Orchestra, one of the successors to Miller. The song's melody was actually created as a student exercise while Miller, who was both an excellent trombonist and arranger, was working with bandleader Ray Noble in 1935. Two sets of lyrics, "Now I Lay Me Down to Weep," by Edward Heyman, and "Gone with the Dawn," by George T. Simon, did not work out well. However, in 1939, Mitchell Parish (1900-1993) devised an appropriate set of lyrics, giving the classic song a classic title. Ironically, Parish's lyrics are seldom heard today. The same is true of the 1929 lyrics he wrote for Hoagy Carmichael's "Stardust" (1927), and somewhat true for the lyrics he supplied in 1933 for Duke Ellington's "Sophisticated Lady," the 1939 lyrics for Peter DeRose's "Deep Purple" (1934), and the 1950 lyrics for Leroy Anderson's "Sleigh Ride" (1948).

"Moonlight Serenade" also was the embodiment of the unique and splendid Miller sound, which emphasized the reeds, with a clarinet dominating over four saxophones. The sound was deliberately created in 1935 while Miller was with Noble, not by accident after Miller had his own ensemble, as portrayed in *The Glenn Miller Story*. In spite of that mistake, and a few others, the film was a very good one, in part because of the fine portrayals by Stewart and Allyson, as well as the exceptional score by Mancini who later was to create his own dreamy love ballad with "moon" in the title, "Moon River" (1961), with lyricist Johnny Mercer.

HARRY JAMES
(THE HARRY JAMES ORCHESTRA, 1939-1983)

Ciribiribin

One of the better recordings by the Glenn Miller Orchestra was "Juke Box Saturday Night." The 1942 song by lyricist Al Stillman and composer Paul McGrane, though not a smash hit or a classic, was quite interesting because of two simulations of the styles of top musicians of the time. One imitation was of the African-American vocal group the Ink Spots, and the other was of Harry James performing his usual virtuosity on the trumpet. The song the James imitator played was "Ciribiribin," one of the themes of the Harry James Orchestra.

That piece, with the tongue-twisting title with five "i"s, was created by Italian lyricist Rudolf Thaler and Italian composer Alberto Pestalozza (1851-1934) in 1898, and it was revived by James in 1943, using new lyrics by Jack Lawrence. Perhaps the number most associated with James, "Ciribiribin" is a sweet, rhythmic, melodic work without the slightest touch of swing-style music in it, despite its being a top number in the 1940s. This was in contrast to the several songs written by Harry Hagg James (1916-1983), who was born in Albany, Georgia, of circus parents. (His father taught him to play the trumpet.)

James wrote the jazz standard "One O'Clock Jump" (1938), with fellow bandleader Count Basie, who adopted it as his lively theme, as well as its sequel "Two O'Clock Jump" (1941), with Basie and Benny Goodman. He also created "I'm Beginning to See the Light" (1945) with Duke Ellington, Johnny Hodges, and Don George, which James's ensemble turned into a number-one hit. James also collaborated on other lesser-known swing pieces: "Life Goes to a Party" (1937), with Benny Goodman; "Peckin'" (1937), with Ben Pollack; "Every Day of My Life" (1939), with Morty Beck and Billy Hays; "Trumpet Blues" (1942) and "Jump Town" (1943), with Jack Matthias; "Everything but You" (1945), words by George, music by Ellington and James; and "The Music Makers" (1941), words by Don Raye, music by James. The last song did not last long, as with many other compositions of the swing era, but it definitely had a title that was very descriptive of that most fertile artistic period in American cultural history.

I've Heard That Song Before

"(It Seems to Me) I've Heard That Song Before" probably has been the sentiment of many listeners to the many songs by famous wordsmith Sammy Cahn (born Samuel Cohen) (1913-1992) and renowned composer Jule Styne (1905-1994). Together and with others, Cahn and Styne have enriched American popular music to a greater degree than most songwriters. One of their efforts was the aforementioned "I've Heard That Song Before," created by Cahn and Styne for the 1942 film *Youth on Parade* and introduced by Frank Sinatra.

A favorite of the Harry James Orchestra, "I've Heard" was recorded with vocalist Helen Forrest. Another more famous piece by Cahn and Styne was "It's Been a Long, Long Time" (1945), recorded by the James ensemble with vocalist Kitty Kallen. This 1945 standard, with the delightful lines "Kiss me once, and kiss me twice, and kiss me once again" was another James favorite. (It also was a favorite of a certain author who got a touch of frostbite when acting out the song during deep winter in college days in cold Connecticut.)

Yet another James favorite by Styne, this time with lyricist Frank Loesser, who was to become a famous lyricist and composer not long after, was the 1941 hit "I Don't Want to Walk Without You," again recorded with Helen Forrest. Styne cowrote that piece before he began his fruitful collaboration with Cahn in 1942. Cahn's first collaborator was Saul Chaplin (born Saul Kaplan). With bandleader Jimmie Lunceford, Cahn and Chaplin created Lunceford's theme "Rhythm Is Our Business" (1935). Even more notable was Cahn and Chaplin's adaptation of a Yiddish song into the 1937 smash hit "Bei Mir Bist Du Schoen." A rage at the time, the appealing Yiddish-English novelty was recorded by the Andrews Sisters and performed at Carnegie Hall by Benny Goodman.

There were a lot of notable names in this one short essay, reflecting the creative energy of the period.

Sleepy Lagoon

Whether it's called "Valse Serenade" or "(By the) Sleepy Lagoon," the 1930 composition by English light classical composer Eric Coates (1886-1957) does not suggest a high degree of energy or rapid rhythm. A dreamy delight, it was adopted as a favorite number of the Harry James Orchestra with its revival in 1942. Lyricist Jack Lawrence (1912-) supplied a set of lyrics for the revival along with a new title, "Sleepy Lagoon." (Another "sleep" song associated with a big band is "Sleep" (1923), by Earl Lebieg, the theme of the Fred Waring Orchestra.)

Lawrence also wrote or collaborated on several other good swing era songs, including the following: "If I Didn't Care" (1939), the smooth low-key theme of the Ink Spots, by himself; "Sunrise Serenade" (1939), with composer Frankie Carle; "All or Nothing at All" (1939), with Arthur Altman, a smash hit in 1940 because of the fine recording by Frank Sinatra; "Linda" (1944), with Ann Ronell; "Tenderly" (1946), with composer Walter Gross; and the words for the dramatic and exciting ballad "Beyond the Sea" (1947), with the music obtained from French composer Charles Trenet.

The contributions by Coates to American popular culture were also significant, in spite of his being born in England. In addition to indirectly supplying a top number for Harry James, Coates wrote several other pieces of some impact in the United States: "Bird Songs at Eventide" (1926), words by Royden Barrie, music by Coates; "I Pitch My Lonely Caravan at Night" (1921), words and music by Coates and Annette Horey; and the compelling light classical work "Knightsbridge March" (1933), from his "London Suite." From "Knightsbridge," Coates's best-known composition, came the melody to accompany American Irving Caesar's lyrics for "Goodbye, Au Revoir, Auf Wiedersehen" (1936). For some reason, this last paragraph has caused this author to want to go to bed and dream of sleepy lagoons.

You Made Me Love You

The old expression "something old, something new, something borrowed, something blue" relates to brides on their wedding day. It may have applied to the beautiful blonde actress and favorite World War II era pinup Betty Grable when she married the famous bandleader Harry James. It also definitely applied to swing era musician James. He used old songs, new songs, borrowed songs, and blue songs in the very successful repertory of the Harry James Orchestra.

One of his numbers that, in a way, fit all four aspects of the saying was "You Made Me Love You." An old classic written in 1913 by lyricist Joe McCarthy (1885-1943) and composer James V. Monaco (1885-1945), "You Made Me" was turned into a new classic by James's brilliantly plaintive, or "blue," trumpet solos. Without borrowing the lyrics, James converted the song into one of the swing era's most notable and familiar pieces. James sort of borrowed "You Made Me" from vocalist Al Jolson, who first made it famous in the 1913 Broadway production *The Honeymoon Express*. The number became one of James's themes, and his trumpet technique was widely borrowed by others.

With a highly successful band and a charming wife, James did much more than just get by. Yet one of his favorite numbers was "I'll Get By (As Long As I Have You)," also borrowed from an earlier time. Written in 1928 by lyricist Roy Turk and musician Fred E. Ahlert, "I'll Get By" was recorded with vocalist Dick Haymes (rhymes with James) in 1941. Another top disc of the time was "I Had the Craziest Dream" (1943), recorded by James, with vocalist Helen Forrest. The 1943 composition, by two notable songwriters, lyricist Mack Gordon and musician Harry Warren, was not their best collaboration. A bit of its appeal at the time, however, may have been due to the crazy dreams many servicemen had when they admired the famous leggy photo of Betty Grable in their lockers, on their walls, or in their memories.

HENRY BUSSE
(THE HENRY BUSSE ORCHESTRA, 1937-1955)

Hot Lips

Is it just coincidence that "buss" is a slang expression for "kiss" and that the opening theme of bandleader Henry Busse (1894-1955) was "Hot Lips"? On the other hand, "Hot Lips" could also apply to an active performance on a trumpet or other brass instrument, as exemplied in the fast-paced trumpet solo in "Hot Lips," the jazz song, or the title could have no particular semantic significance to Busse's life or career. However, it did have an artistic significance to the Henry Busse Orchestra, as did his closing theme, "When Day Is Done" (1926), words by Bud DeSylva, music by Robert Katscher.

Created in 1922 by Busse, Henry Lange, and Lou Davis, memorable "Hot Lips" was recorded in 1934. Busse, born in Magdeburg, Germany, also collaborated on one of the better blues numbers, "The Wang, Wang Blues" (1921), with Gus Mueller and "Buster" Johnson writing the lyrics and Busse devising the plaintive melody to accompany their lines. "Wang, Wang," which slowly oozes out a feeling of breathless despair and gloom, is a marked contrast to the upbeat and rapid-rhythm "Hot Lips," which leaves listeners and performers almost breathless, but happy.

Another number of importance to the Busse ensemble was "With Plenty of Money and You" (1936), words by Al Dubin, music by

Harry Warren, which was inserted in the film *Gold Diggers of 1937* and recorded by Busse. Dubin and Warren were associated with a number of successful songs in the 1930s, including the classic "Lullaby of Broadway," for which Dubin also wrote the lyrics and Warren the music. That piece won an Academy Award for its presentation in the movie musical *Gold Diggers of 1935*. With so much gold in the titles of films for which they wrote, and so much gold figuratively received for their songs, Dubin and Warren were on the money when they predicted in one of their early (1933) collaborations, "We're in the Money." By 1936, it was easy and realistic for the duo to claim "plenty of money."

JAN SAVITT
(THE JAN SAVITT ORCHESTRA, EARLY 1930s-1948)

Make Believe Island

Similar to other forms of entertainment, the music of the big bands helped the listener willingly participate in make-believe events and places. By adopting "Make Believe Island" as a favorite number, the Jan Savitt Orchestra may have been partially admitting its role as a catalyst for dreams and fantasies.

Written in 1940 by lyricists Nick Kenny (1895-1975), Charles Kenny (1898-?), and Sam Coslow (1902-) and composer Will Grosz (1894-1939), "Make Believe" was a fine collaboration by four songwriters of modest to moderate achievement. The Kennys also wrote the following numbers: the enduring ballad "Love Letters in the Sand" (1931), the theme of the George Hall Orchestra, with musician J. Fred Coots; the theme of the Joe Venuti Orchestra, "Last Night," or "Why Couldn't It Last Last Night?" (1939), with musician Austen Croom-Johnson; and the lesser-known songs "Cathedral in the Pines" (1938), "Gone Fishin'" (1950), "Leanin' on the Ole Top Rail" (1939), "There's a Gold Mine in the Sky" (1937), and "While a Cigarette Was Burning" (1938), with each other. Coots also collaborated with lyricist Sam M. Lewis on "One Minute to One" (1933), the theme of the Gray Gordon Orchestra.

Coslow also wrote many other numbers: "If I Were King" (1930), with Newall Chase and Leo Robin; "True Blue Lou"

(1929), with Robin and Richard A. Whiting; "Cocktails for Two" (1934), with Arthur Johnston, the main theme song of Spike Jones and his City Slickers (another Jones theme was "The Sheik of Araby" [1921], words by Harry B. Smith and Francis Wheeler, music by Ted Snyder); "Sing You Sinners" (1930), words by Coslow, music by W. Franke Harling; "Je Vous Aime" (1947, by Coslow); and after-the-fact lyrics for Edward Confrey's 1921 piano piece "Kitten on the Keys."

Grosz (also known as Hugh Williams) also created other songs: "Along the Santa Fe Trail" (1940), with Al Dubin and Edwina Coolidge; "In an Old Dutch Garden" (1939), with Mack Gordon, who teamed with composer Harry Revel to produce the theme of the Paul Neighbors Orchestra, "Love Thy Neighbor" (1924); and "At the Cafe Continental" (1936), "Bird on the Wing" (1936), "Harbor Lights" (1937), "Poor Little Angeline" (1936), "Ten Pretty Girls" (1934), plus the enduring "Red Sails in the Sunset" (1935), all with Jimmy Kennedy.

With the large variety of pleasant allusions in the songs of Nick and Charles Kenny, Sam Coslow, and Will Grosz, it would be very easy to slip into the happy illusions of make-believe. As one of Savitt's theme songs, a 1931 composition by lyricist Oscar Hammerstein II and composer Sigmund Romberg, suggests, "It's a Wonderful World."

720 in the Books

It seems perfectly normal that a violinist born in St. Petersburg, Russia, should adopt a string-dominated excerpt from a masterpiece by a great Russian composer. So when Jan Savitt, along with Al Hoffman, modified the romantic and dreamy main theme of Peter Ilich Tchaikovsky's 1893 Symphony No. 6 (the *Pathetique*) into the popular 1941 song "Now and Forever," it should not have been particularly surprising. However, for a Russian whose father played in Tsar Nicholas II's Imperial Regiment Band to become the leader of a jazz-oriented orchestra in the United States is a far from natural and obvious transition.

Yet Jan Savitt (1913-1948) did develop into the head of the notable Jan Savitt Orchestra and, in the process, provided some of the ensemble's musical material. The most notable composition by Savitt is perhaps "720 in the Books" (1939), a bit of a classic of the era. The odd-titled "720" was the product of a collaboration between Savitt, John G. Watson (1912-1977), and Harold Adamson (1906-). (Another song by Savitt and Jimmy Schultz has an interesting title, the 1937 instrumental "Quaker City Jazz," which was the theme of Jan Savitt and his Top Hatters.) Watson also wrote a few other songs, including "Goodnight to You All" (1937), with Muriel Watson, and "Racing with the Moon" (1941), with Vaughn Monroe and Pauline Pope (the theme of the Vaughn Monroe Orchestra). Among other things, Adamson wrote the lyrics for the theme of the *I Love Lucy* television series (1951) two years after Eliot Daniel wrote the music. That song was the theme of the Desi Arnaz Orchestra.

Other favorite numbers of Savitt included "El Rancho Grande," or "My Ranch" (1934), original Spanish lyrics and music by Silvano R. Ramos, English lyrics by Bartley Costello, and "Tuxedo Junction" (1940) by lyricist Buddy Feyne and composers Erskine Hawkins, William Johnson, and Julian Dash. The latter number was a top favorite of the Erskine Hawkins Orchestra and also recorded by the Glenn Miller and Benny Goodman Orchestras. Add to the six orchestras noted thus far (Savitt, Monroe, Arnaz, Hawkins, Miller, and Goodman) the orchestras of Charlie Barnet, Glen Gray, Sammy Kaye, Tommy Reynolds, Claude Thornhill, and probably more who also recorded Savitt's "720 in the Books," and you get about a dozen big bands in the historical books.

JIMMIE LUNCEFORD (THE JIMMIE LUNCEFORD ORCHESTRA, 1927-1947)

The Organ Grinder's Swing

The mechanical music emitted from the hand-cranked hurdy-gurdies that used to be common in Europe and the United States could be quite appealing, especially if a lively monkey accompanied the organ grinder. But it did not have the swing style, designed for dancing, that used to be so prevalent in the United States and elsewhere. This is perhaps the main reason for the appeal of the title "The Organ Grinder's Swing" (1936), one of the favorite numbers of the Jimmie Lunceford Orchestra.

The main reason for the song's success, however, was its delightful music by Will Hudson. Even more successful than "Organ Grinder" was Hudson's "Moonglow" (1934), written with lyricists Irving Mills and Eddie DeLange, which was a favorite number of the Benny Goodman Orchestra. (Mills [1894-1985] also collaborated on the lyrics of "Organ Grinder" with noted lyricist Mitchell Parish [1900-1993] and wrote several well-known songs with longtime associate Duke Ellington.) Hudson also wrote the lesser-known instrumental "Jazznocracy" (1934), one of Lunceford's themes.

While "The Organ Grinder's Swing" strongly suggested dance music, another Jimmie Lunceford (1902-1947) favorite clearly stated that it was intended for dancers. Sy Oliver, who played the trumpet in Lunceford's band for several years, wrote the melody of

"For Dancers Only" in 1937, with lyrics supplied by Don Raye and Vic Schoen. Oliver's rhythmic fox-trot was also a favorite of the Bob Crosby Orchestra, which recorded it in 1939, about two years after Lunceford did. From the numbers most preferred by Lunceford, "Swing" and "For Dancers Only," plus one of his themes, "Rhythm Is Our Business" (1935), by Lunceford, Sammy Cahn, and Saul Chaplin, it is apparent that Lunceford loved to provide highly danceable music. Although some of the arrangements he used had an odd sort of swing style, he did help many thousands of feet move to a bouncy beat for years.

Rhythm Is Our Business

Rhythm was the business of the well-known African-American bandleader Jimmie Lunceford. Born James Melvin Lunceford in Fulton, Missouri, he led the Jimmie Lunceford Orchestra, one of the more disciplined and distinguished jazz ensembles of the 1930s and 1940s. Lunceford was also a composer of consequence, though he generally left the arrangements for his orchestra during the peak years of 1935 to 1937 to trumpet player Sy Oliver and pianist Edwin Wilcox.

"Rhythm" was also prominently featured in the titles of two notable compositions to which Lunceford contributed: "Rhythm Is Our Business" (1935), one of the themes of Lunceford, was cowritten with Sammy Cahn and Saul Chaplin. Cahn and Don Raye wrote the lyrics and Lunceford and Chaplin created the music for the second "rhythm" number, "(If I Had) Rhythm in My Nursery Rhymes" (1935). Incidentally, the best-known collaboration by Cahn (1913-1992) and Chaplin (1912-1997), also known as Saul Kaplan, was "Bei Mir Bist Du Schoen" (1937). It was a smash of the big band era, primarily because of its very appealing rhythm. A third Lunceford composition, created by him alone, was "Uptown Blues," a 1930s instrumental that became one of his themes.

Although Lunceford was proficient in a wide range of reed instruments, which he played with other groups before starting his own orchestra, he never played any instrument with his own ensemble, with one exception. When his band recorded "Liza" (1929, words by Ira Gershwin and Gus Kahn, music by George Gershwin), Lunceford played a wind instrument, the flute. Perhaps one of the reasons the Jimmie Lunceford Orchestra was among the elite of the swing era was Lunceford's general avoidance of activities that might divert his attention and energy from being a top-notch leader.

JIMMY DORSEY
(THE JIMMY DORSEY ORCHESTRA,
1935-1953)

Besame Mucho

Jimmy Dorsey (1904-1957), who played both the saxophone and the clarinet, also selected numbers from both American and foreign sources. Jimmy's main repository for overseas songs was Spanish-speaking cultures. Some of his orchestra's favorite pieces originally came from the fertile fields of these nations that have supplied, along with Portuguese-speaking Brazil, so many fine works for consumption in the United States.

The lush and rhythmic song "Besame Mucho" ("Kiss Me Much") was one of Jimmy's top hits. Written by Consuelo Velazquez (Spanish words and music), "Besame" was a top seller in 1944, with English lyrics supplied by Sunny Skylar. (Some years later, in 1958, Skylar wrote lyrics for Felix Arndt's 1916 instrumental "Nola," which was the theme of the Vincent Lopez Orchestra.) Three other hits for Jimmy were "Yours," or "Quiéreme Mucho" (1931), Spanish words by Augustin Rodriguez, English words by Jack Sherr, music by Gonzalo Roig (the theme of singer Vera Lynn, revived in 1941); "Amapola," or "Pretty Little Poppy" (1924), by Joseph M. Lacalle, who wrote the music and both Spanish lyrics and one set of English lyrics; and "Green Eyes" (1929), originally "Aquellos Ojos Verdes." The Spanish lyrics for the latter winner, which was revived in 1941, were by Adolfo Utrera, the English lyrics were by L. Wolfe Gilbert, and the music was by Nilo Menendez.

Another set of English lyrics for Dorsey's revival of "Amapola" was by Albert Gamse, and another top song by lyricist Gilbert was "Waiting for the Robert E. Lee" (1912), created with composer Lewis F. Muir. With dual instruments, dual languages, dual hits, dual appearances of songs (original and revivals), and even dual sets of translated lyrics, the reader may be tired of anything resembling the number two. Yet, it should be mentioned that Skylar, who wrote the English lyrics for the 1944 hit "Besame Mucho," also did the same for another Spanish-language song that was a success in the same year. That piece was "Amor," music by Gabriel Ruiz and Spanish lyrics by someone with a compound surname, Ricardo López Méndez. Stretching the analogy even more, Ruiz wrote the music for a second hit in 1947, "Cuanto Le Gusta," with English lyrics supplied by another Gilbert, Ray. Let's stop here. Enough is enough!

Contrasts

Several contrasts are applicable to the life and work of the noted bandleader Jimmy Dorsey. In addition to the various contrasts between him and his brother Tommy, Jimmy actually wrote a number with the title "Contrasts." First created in 1933 as a solo for saxophonist Jimmy, with the appealing title "Oodles of Noodles," the piece was a hit for the Dorsey Brothers Orchestra. It was a hit again in 1941 when arranged into an orchestral work with the contrasting title. The theme of the Jimmy Dorsey Orchestra, along with another number later adopted as a closing theme, "So Rare" (1937, words by Jack Sharpe, music by Jerry Herst), "Contrasts"/"Oodles of Noodles" brings up another contrast. One of the themes mentions rarity, and the other ("Oodles") suggests abundance. Also, when Dorsey made a hit out of another kind of food, it was the highly contrasting "Tangerine" (1942, words by Johnny Mercer, music by Victor Schertzinger).

One of the other favorite numbers of the Jimmy Dorsey ensemble was "Is It True What They Say About Dixie?" "Dixie" was created by lyricists Irving Caesar and Sammy Lerner with composer Gerald Marks in 1936. Marks also created the Frank Sinatra hit "All of Me" (1931), with lyricist Seymour Simons, and Caesar, in contrast, had several more top songs. With composer Vincent Youmans, Caesar wrote "I Want to be Happy" (1925), "Sometimes I'm Happy (1927), and the classic "Tea for Two" (1924). He also cowrote another classic, "Swanee" (1919), with the great George Gershwin, a rare genius who died prematurely the same year Dorsey's theme "So Rare" was created.

So Rare

In November 1956, the Jimmy Dorsey Orchestra (using the personnel of his brother Tommy's former band) made a hit recording of "So Rare" (1937), the group's closing theme. (The words of this fine number were by Jack Sharpe and the music by Jerry Herst.) It was indeed a rare moment for any ensemble led by Jimmy, none of which had had a hit for several years. (Even some of Jimmy's successful recordings, for example, the World War II era ballad "They're Either Too Young or Too Old" [1943], by proven songwriters Arthur Schwartz and Frank Loesser, sung by popular Kitty Kallen, were quite transitory.) Ironically, Jimmy died a few months later, before the "So Rare" recording was released in 1957, taking some of the bloom off this notable achievement.

Upon his death, Jimmy, although his original 1935-1953 ensemble was definitely eclipsed by his brother Tommy's, left behind a very notable musical legacy. One way in which Jimmy surpassed his better-known younger brother, who preceded him in death by about six months, was in song composition. Whereas Tommy wrote little that has come down to us, Jimmy did write two pieces of some consequence. In 1941, Jimmy and Paul Madeira collaborated on the very pleasant ballad "I'm Glad There Is You," or "In This World of Ordinary People," a significant hit for the Jimmy Dorsey Orchestra. In the same year, Jimmy's theme song, the 1933 saxophone solo "Oodles of Noodles," arranged for orchestra and renamed "Contrasts," was also a hit.

While "So Rare" could obviously apply to Jimmy's two compositions, it also, along with "so good," could be used as a label for the overall quality of his exceptional ensemble. That was the basic message of the 1947 film *The Fabulous Dorseys*. Although an interesting movie, *The Fabulous Dorseys* was not as filled with the music of the two brothers as one might think. Apparently, in deference to the 1935 split between the two, Tommy's two themes,

"Opus One" (1944, music by Sy Oliver) and "I'm Getting Sentimental Over You" (1933, words by Ned Washington, music by
George Bassman), and Jimmy's theme, "Contrasts," were not performed in the film. This was somewhat of a shame, for such oppor-
tunities to honor musicians of this caliber in film are indeed so rare.

JOHN KIRBY
(THE JOHN KIRBY ORCHESTRA, 1937-1947)

Bounce of the Sugar Plum Fairy

If the title "Bounce of the Sugar Plum Fairy" sounds vaguely familiar, it is because the piece was adapted from a very famous composition, "Dance of the Sugar Plum Fairy." The original, of course, was one of the highlights of the famous and enduring ballet *The Nutcracker* (1892), by the great Russian composer Peter Ilich Tchaikovsky (1840-1893). Even stranger than the title was the conversion, by saxophonist Harold "Hal" Singer (1919-), of this delicate classical number into a swing era jazz number.

The John Kirby Orchestra, with a light, breezy, ingenious style, recorded "Bounce" in 1941, as well as other classically derived pieces in the same period. The other adaptations of "serious music" by the Kirby group included "Anitra's Dance" from *Peer Gynt Suite No. 1* (1876), by Norwegian composer Edvard Grieg (1843-1907); a sextet from the opera *Lucia di Lammermoor* (1835), by Italian composer Gaetano Donizetti (1797-1848); "Humoresque" (1894) by Czech composer Antonin Dvořák (1841-1904); and "Serenade" or "Hark, Hark, the Lark" (1826) by Austrian composer Franz Schubert (1797-1828).

In spite of all these nineteenth-century European classics in the Kirby repertory, classics from the twentieth century and the United

States were not ignored. One of the all-time great jazz numbers, "Sweet Georgia Brown" was recorded in 1939. Written in 1925 by Ben Bernie, Maceo Pinkard, and Kenneth Casey, "Georgia Brown" was also a favorite of Bernie's sweet band. As with the adaptation from Tchaikovsky, it certainly had a large amount of bounce.

Undecided

Not all of the swing era bands were big bands, that is, ensembles with fifteen or more performers. For example, the John Kirby Orchestra was actually a sextet, or a small band. Two of the players in this group were John Kirby, string bass and leader, and Charlie Shavers, trumpet.

Kirby (1908-1952) was born in Baltimore and became famous as the head of one of the more innovative jazz ensembles of the 1930s and 1940s and one of the first African-American bands to be widely accepted. Shavers (1917-1971) was born in New York City and was a composer and arranger as well as a skilled performer. He played with the Red Norvo Orchestra, whose theme was "I Surrender Dear" (1932, words by Gordon Clifford, music by Harry Barris), and with the Raymond Scott Orchestra, whose theme was "Toy Trumpet" (1937, words by Sidney D. Mitchell, music by Lew Pollack). Shavers' most notable composition was "Undecided" (1939), words by Sid Robin, music by Shavers. With its catchy beat and memorable lines, "First you say you do, and then you don't, and then you say you will, and then you won't," "Undecided" became one of Kirby's greatest successes. Lyricist Robin (1912-   ) also wrote the words for "Flying Home" (1939), the theme of bandleader Lionel Hampton. Hampton and another noted bandleader, Benny Goodman, collaborated on the music.

Shavers also wrote "Pastel Blue," a 1939 hit instrumental, with Artie Shaw, which changed to "Why Begin Again?" when lyrics were added in 1943 by Don Raye, and "20th-Century Closet" (1940), a fox-trot created with Kirby. Other fox-trot recordings made by Kirby include "Rose Room," or "In Sunny Roseland" (1917), words and music by Harry Williams and Art Hickman, and "(I Wanna Go Where You Go, Do What You Do) Then I'll Be Happy" (1925), words by Sidney Clare and Lew Brown, music by Cliff Friend. That friendly song certainly does not exhibit the slightest touch of indecision.

LARRY CLINTON
(THE LARRY CLINTON ORCHESTRA,
1938-1941, 1948-1950)

Deep Purple

Part of Larry Clinton's (1909-) success as a bandleader was his choice of music for the Larry Clinton Orchestra. Among his favorite numbers were two popular classics, "Deep Purple" and "Heart and Soul." "Deep Purple" was originally a beautiful moody piano piece created by Peter DeRose (1900-1953) in 1934. In 1935, "Purple" was arranged for orchestra and, in 1939, received a good set of lyrics by noted wordsmith Mitchell Parish (1900-1993). "Heart and Soul" (1938), a pulsating, brooding number, was written by two outstanding songwriters, lyricist Frank Loesser and musician Hoagy Carmichael. Both of these winning numbers are noted for their deep tones.

However, there was nothing deep about the wafting romantic strains of "Martha," or "Marta," a Clinton favorite. Written in 1931 by Moses Simon and L. Wolfe Gilbert, the song told the story of the "rambling rose of the wildwood." The same tonal characteristics apply to another Clinton hit, "Johnson Rag." Very lively "Johnson" was written as an instrumental in 1917 by Guy Hall and Henry Kleinauf, but after it was revived in the midst of the swing era, it slowed down long enough to acquire some 1940 lyrics by Jack Lawrence.

Of course, the revival of "Johnson Rag" meant reaching back over a generation, or a bit deep into history. Clinton dug considerably deeper into the past for the theme of another deep-toned favorite, "Shadrack (Meshack Abednego)." Although written in 1931 by Robert MacGimsey, who also created a good Christmas song, "Sweet Little Jesus Boy" (1934), the novelty was based on an incident in the Old Testament. According to the book of Daniel, Shadrach, Meshach, and Abednego were cast into a fiery furnace but were saved by an angel. Not every big band number is involved with deep theological matters.

My Reverie

Although Larry Clinton apparently has no direct connection with the president with the same last name, he had artistic associations with two famous classical composers. From the music of Claude Debussy (1862-1918), specifically the French composer's piano piece *Rêverie* (1890), he created "My Reverie" (1938), one of the themes of the Larry Clinton Orchestra. From the music of Peter Ilich Tchaikovsky (1840-1893), specifically the Russian composer's famous overture *Romeo and Juliet* (1870), Clinton and Buddy Bernier created "Our Love" (1939), another Clinton favorite. In both cases, Clinton sustained the moods of the original compositions, the dreaminess of Debussy and the romance of Tchaikovsky.

But Clinton did not just borrow from others. Born in Brooklyn, New York, he became a trumpet player and arranger without any appreciable outside instruction. Having more success with arranging than performance, working with several bands in the 1930s, Clinton naturally progressed to composition. In addition to the two aforementioned classically influenced works, Clinton created three completely original songs of note. The most memorable of these is the playful "Dipsy Doodle" (1937, words and music by Clinton), one of Clinton's themes. Also of consequence is Clinton's 1937 instrumental "Study in Brown," his signature theme.

Less known is Clinton's "Satan Takes a Holiday" (1937). When coupled with another Clinton hit, "Shadrack (Meshack Abednego)" (1931), by Robert MacGimsey, which was based on a biblical passage about three men cast in a fiery furnace, "Satan" provided as much theology as any big band dared to cast into song. Most swing numbers took holidays from anything religious or philosophical.

LES BROWN
(THE LES BROWN ORCHESTRA, 1938-1970s)

Joltin' Joe DiMaggio

Several Hall of Fame baseball players have been honored by songs. Most of these compositions, in contrast with the players, were not especially notable. In the early 1950s, "Say Hey" was written for Willie Mays, and in the mid-1950s, "Did You See Jackie Robinson Hit That Ball?" was played by the Count Basie Orchestra and "I Love Mickey" was created for Mickey Mantle. By far the best known of this type of song was "Joltin' Joe DiMaggio," which extolled the prowess of the "Yankee Clipper," the slugger who preceded Mantle as the big bat of the New York Yankees.

"Joltin' Joe," which had a strident or somewhat jolting tempo to match the power and drama of the game, was created by lyricist Alan Courtney and composer Ben Homer (1917-1975). It was a big hit by the Les Brown Orchestra, with vocalist Betty Bonney, in 1941. Homer also collaborated on another Les Brown favorite, the markedly differently styled "Sentimental Journey" (1944), with Brown and Bud Green.

Other numbers for Les Brown (1912-) and his "band of renown" included the following: the tender "Twilight Time" (1944), by Buck Ram, Artie Dunn, Al Nevins, and Morty Nevins; the romantic "Ramona" (1927), words by L. Wolfe Gilbert, music by Muriel Wayne; the now forgotten "Midnight Sun" (1947), words by

Johnny Mercer, music by Francis J. Burke; the smooth "Dream" (1944), by Mercer; the homey "Back in Your Own Back Yard" (1927), by Al Jolson, Billy Rose, and Dave Dreyer; the sophisticated "It's All Right with Me" (1953), by Cole Porter; the jazzy and wordless "Slaughter on Tenth Avenue" (1936), music by Richard Rodgers; the dynamic "I've Got My Love to Keep Me Warm" (1937), by Irving Berlin; and the very charming Doris Day hit "My Dreams Are Getting Better All the Time" (1944), by Vic Mizzy and Mann Curtis.

Mizzy and Curtis later wrote "The Jones Boy," which captivated audiences in 1953. The "Jones Boy," though a pleasant piece, did not keep the attention of the American public for very long, whereas the versatile Mays, the pioneering Robinson, the boyish Mantle, and the almost regal DiMaggio and other very talented "boys of summer" will be remembered as long as their sport is.

Sentimental Journey

One of the theme songs of the Les Brown Orchestra was the now obscure "Leap Frog" (1941), words by Leo Corday, music by Joe Garland. Another much more famous theme song of Brown was "Sentimental Journey," written in 1944 by Brown, Ben Homer (1917-1975), and Bud Green (1897-   ), and recorded with great success in 1945 by attractive young vocalist Doris Day. Although probably the best-known number associated with Lester Raymond Brown, who was born in Reinerton, Pennsylvania, slow and smooth "Sentimental," a World War II era favorite, was not the only composition to which he contributed. In 1963, Brown, John D. Loudermilk, Bob Gibson, and Albert Stanton produced western-flavored "Abilene," based on an old folk song. Brown also wrote a 1937 instrumental, "Dance of the Blue Devils," which he used as a theme. One more Brown theme was "Shangri-la" (1946), by Matt Malneck and Robert Maxwell.

One of Brown's collaborators on "Sentimental," Bud Green, was even more active in the composition business. He wrote the following numbers: the southward chugging "Alabamy Bound" (1925), with colyricist Bud DeSylva and composer Ray Henderson; another song of the South, "Away Down South in Heaven" (1927), and the romantic and reciprocal "I Love My Baby—My Baby Loves Me" (1925), with composer Harry Warren; the salute "Congratulations" (1929) with Maceo Pinkard, Coleman Goetz, and Sam H. Stept; the command "Do Something" (1929) and the complaint "That's My Weakness Now" (1928), with Stept; the promise "I'll Always Be in Love with You" (1929), with Harry Ruby; the time-constrained, but not artistically constrained, "Once in a While" (1937), words by Green, music by Michael Edwards; the song about a city in New York apparently chosen just for its rhyme, "He's a Gypsy from Poughkeepsie" (1937), with Emery Deutsch; and the "F" song "Flat Foot Floogie (with the Floy Floy)" (1938), with Slim Gaillard and Sam Stewart.

So Green not only had a sentimental journey but a long and profitable artistic one. He may have tripped a bit over the tongue-twisting five "F" "Flat Foot Floogie," which was written a few years before World War II, during which "4-F" was not a label of pride. Still, he and Brown were significant artists of their time.

LIONEL HAMPTON
(THE LIONEL HAMPTON
ORCHESTRA, 1940-1980s,
STILL OCCASIONALLY TOURING)

After You've Gone

One of the better numbers of the 1930s was "When Your Lover Has Gone," a sad and succulent song written in 1931 by little-known composer Einar A. Swan. Similar to so many compositions about lost or unattainable loves, it could very well be described as a torch song or even sort of a blues song. An equally effective ballad of the same general mood that also contains the woeful word "gone" was "After You've Gone" (1918), created by Henry Creamer and J. Turner Layton. A favorite of the swing era, at least three big names in the jazz field, Count Basie, Benny Goodman, and Lionel Hampton, recorded it.

African-American Hampton (1909-), born in Louisville, Kentucky, was most famous for his virtuoso performances on the vibraphone, also known popularly as the "vibes." He was the first jazz musician to extensively utilize this percussion instrument, and the songs he favored, such as the slow-paced "After You've Gone," tended to be ones suitable for the vibraphone. It is uncertain, however, whether the creators of "After You've Gone," Creamer and Layton, ever envisioned their composition being played on a vibraphone, or even being a jazz standard.

Furthermore, if you look at some of their other songs, for example, "The Bombo-Shay" (1917), with Henry Lewis; "Dear Old Southland" (1921), based on the African-American spiritual "Deep River" (published 1875); "Sweet Emalina, My Gal" (1917); and "Way Down Yonder in New Orleans" (1922), none of them, with the possible exception of "Way Down Yonder," have the feel of a true jazz number. However, just about anything can be adapted to the hard-to-define genre we call jazz. Creamer and Layton were holdovers from an earlier time when jazz and big bands were not kings of American culture. Their atypical jazz favorite almost seemed to be saying to the duo, after you've gone the way of most popular entertainers, I will be around for yet another generation. Yet "Way Down Yonder" has lasted way longer as a public favorite, and still is heard today. Both fine pieces, however, have given many audiences good "vibes" over the years.

Flying Home

Most persons who have heard John Philip Sousa's famous "Washington Post March" (1889) probably realize that the danceable march was written in honor of a big-city newspaper. In contrast, those who hear Lionel Hampton's much less famous jazz work, "Toledo Blade," probably do not know that the piece, whether intended or not, refers to a newspaper in Toledo, Ohio. Recorded in 1956, "Toledo" appeared a decade after what probably was Hampton's most productive period as a composer.

That fertile period, around the end of World War II, provided the Lionel Hampton Orchestra with a substantial amount of material and fame. Hampton's "Dough, Rey, Mi," created with Tommy Southern and Nat King Cole, appeared in 1944. "Hamp's Boogie Woogie," a piece that Hampton played on the piano, appeared in 1945. His "Red Top" appeared around 1947. Best of all, his "He-Ba-Ba-Re-Bop," with Gladys Hampton and Curley Hampton, livened audiences in 1945. Perhaps his most famous work, "He-Ba-Ba-Re-Bop," also known as "Hey! Ba-Ba-Re-Bop," is reminiscent of the energy and spontaneity of early rock compositions. It is the type of work that encourages the active playing of drums, another skill that the versatile Hampton mastered.

The theme of bandleader, composer, vibraphonist, pianist, and drummer Hampton, however, was "Flying Home" (1939). Written with lyricist Sid Robin (1912-) and cocomposer Benny Goodman, "Flying Home" helped keep Hampton flying high for years. The Hampton Orchestra recorded "Flying" with great success in 1942, after Hampton had recorded it with the Goodman sextet. Whether Hampton actually flew home after the 1942 recording is uncertain, and whether he called his birthplace, Louisville, his home, or Chicago, the city in which he grew up, or someplace else, he surely did much airplane traveling when his success in the states allowed for similar overseas tours in Israel, Europe, North Africa, and Australia during the 1956 to 1960 period.

RAY ANTHONY
(THE RAY ANTHONY
ORCHESTRA, 1946-1960s,
THEN WITH A SMALLER GROUP
THROUGH THE 1980s)

At Last

Charles Tobias (1898-1970) and Sam M. Lewis (1885-1959) were both popular American lyricists of note. Since they both supplied lyrics for songs, it would be relatively unusual for them to work together a lot, although long-term collaboration on lyrics has been known to occur. For example, Betty Comden and Adolph Green were colyricists for years, providing good lyrics for two outstanding composers, Leonard Bernstein and Jule Styne.

Another long-term colyricist situation involved the aforementioned Lewis. He teamed with other lyricists for seven songs of consequence. With fellow wordsmith Joe Young, he wrote the following numbers: "Rockabye Your Baby with a Dixie Melody" (1918, composer Jean Schwartz); "How Ya Gonna Keep 'em Down on the Farm?" (1919, composer Walter Donaldson); "My Mammy" (1921, composer Donaldson); "Dinah" (1924, composer Harry Akst); "Five Foot Two, Eyes of Blue" (1925, composer Ray Henderson); and "I'm Sitting on Top of the World" (1925, composer Henderson). In case you are counting, the seventh song will be mentioned soon.

In contrast, Tobias only had two significant colyricist occasions. One of these involved an Andrews Sisters classic, "Don't Sit Under the Apple Tree" (1939), with colyricist Lew Brown and composer Sam H. Stept. The other was a less enduring (and the seventh) song, "At Last" (1935), written with colyricist Lewis and composer Henry Tobias. Although not even approaching the status of a classic, "At Last" was one of the favorite numbers of the Ray Anthony Orchestra, as well as being performed by other ensembles, for instance, the Glenn Miller Orchestra. At last we have come to one of the basic points of this essay.

Certain numbers were embraced and performed by more than one big band. For example, both Ray Anthony (1922-) and Ted Heath recorded Walter Schumann's 1949 "Dragnet," and Anthony, Stan Kenton, and Randy Brooks were among the many who recorded "Harlem Nocturne" (1943). The theme of the Randy Brooks Orchestra, "Harlem" was by lyricist Dick Rogers and musician Earle H. Hagen. That composition, along with "Underneath the Harlem Moon" (1932), by Mack Gordon and Harry Revel, was a mainstream white composition honoring the gathering spot for so many fine African-American musicians and their bands during the 1920s and 1930s.

The Bunny Hop

Ray Anthony, born Raymond Antonini in Bentleyville, Pennsylvania, was a trumpet player and a bandleader of some consequence, becoming particularly notable in the 1950s. (Considering his instrument, it is not surprising that he adopted "Young Man with a Horn" [1944, introduced by Harry James, words by Ralph Freed, music by George Stoll], as his theme. "Young Man" is not to be confused with "Man with a Horn" [1946, by Jack Jenney, Bonnie Lake, and Eddie DeLange], one of the themes of the Boyd Raeburn Orchestra, along with "Over the Rainbow" [1939, words by Edgar Yipsel Harburg, music by Harold Arlen], and "Raeburn's Theme" [recorded 1944, by Raeburn and Eddie Finckel]. Among others, the Steve Allen Orchestra recorded "Man with a Horn." The actual theme of the Jack Jenney Orchestra was another composition by Jenney, "City Night" [1940, written with Joe Wilder and William Engvick].) Anthony also did some composition, for example, "The Bunny Hop." Written by Anthony and Leonard Auletti in 1951, and recorded by the Ray Anthony Orchestra the same year, "Bunny" was one of the dance crazes of the 1950s.

Another even bigger dance rage of that decade was "The Hokey Pokey." Anthony's recording of "Hokey" in 1953 created a sensation that lasted well into the 1990s, "Hokey," with its instructions to leisurely move various body parts, is still performed to a fair extent. Its predecessor, "The Bunny Hop," which requires a lot more energy to perform, was more or less passé by the 1960s. "Hokey" was probably written by Larry LaPrise (1913?-1996), Charles P. Macak, and Tafft Baker around 1948 and recorded in 1949. However, some World War II veterans have claimed that "Hokey" was very popular in England around 1943 and that LaPrise and his associates merely appropriated it.

Although Ray Anthony had big hits with "The Bunny Hop" and "The Hokey Pokey," both dances, he had his greatest success with a march, "Dragnet." Composed in 1949 for the radio series *Dragnet,* and used for the 1951-1959 and 1967-1970 television series of the same name, "Dragnet" turned out to be a smash recording for Anthony in August 1953. The slow, deliberate, and dramatic "Dragnet" theme, also known as "Dragnet March" and "Danger Ahead," was written by American composer and choral conductor Walter Schumann (1913-1958).

Although Harry Truman of Missouri and Dwight Eisenhower of Kansas were presidents of the United States during the 1951-1953 period of triumph for the Ray Anthony Orchestra, the music man from Bentleyville, Pennsylvania, was, for a while, one of the kings of American popular culture.

RUSS MORGAN
(THE RUSS MORGAN ORCHESTRA, 1933-1960s)

Pocketful of Dreams

Songwriters Johnny Burke (1908-1964) and James V. Monaco (1885-1945) created pieces that ranged from near heavenly in style to silly in mood. Perhaps the most heavenly number by either was "You Made Me Love You," especially when performed exquisitely on Harry James's trumpet. ("You Made Me" was created in 1913 by lyricist Joe McCarthy and composer Monaco.) Also close to heavenly was "Misty," the ethereal 1955 ballad by lyricist Burke and composer Erroll Garner. Burke directly mentioned heaven in the 1936 standard "Pennies from Heaven," created with composer Arthur Johnston, and stars in the 1944 Academy Award-winner "Swinging on a Star," created with composer Jimmy Van Heusen.

When writing as a team, Burke and Monaco also mentioned heaven in their 1939 "East Side of Heaven" and a kite trying to get to the heavens in their "Go Fly a Kite" (1939). They also touched on soaring aspirations in their "(I've Got a) Pocketful of Dreams" (1938), created for the Bing Crosby and Fred MacMurray film *Sing You Sinners*. "Pocketful" became one of the favorite numbers of the Russ Morgan Orchestra.

Other compositions by Burke and Monaco were not especially affiliated with the sky or heaven: "An Apple for the Teacher" (1939); "April Played the Fiddle" (1940); "Hang Your Heart on a Hickory

Limb" (1939); "My Heart Is Taking Lessons" (1937); "On the Sentimental Side" (1937); "Only Forever" (1940); "Rhythm on the River"
(1940); "Sweet Potato Piper" (1940); "That Sly Old Gentleman from
Featherbend Lane" (1939); "That's for Me" (1941); and "Too Romantic" (1940). However, another piece by the team of Monaco and
McCarthy that produced the elevating classic "You Made Me Love
You" was the decidedly unelevating "Shave and a Haircut, Bay
Rum" (1914), which was first published in 1914 as "Rum-Diddle-de-
um Bum, That's It." Based on "Hot Scotch Rag" (1911), "Shave and
a Haircut" was revived in the middle of the swing era (1939) and
later provided the melody for the advertising ditty "You'll Get a Kick
out of Kix."

You're Nobody
'Til Somebody Loves You

You can't blame Russ Morgan for adopting "So Tired" as one of his theme songs. Morgan (1904-1969), born in Scranton, Pennsylvania, was a very active musician from a state that produced several other notable active bandleaders, including Ray Anthony, Les Brown, Ted Weems, Billy Eckstine, and Jimmy and Tommy Dorsey. Morgan was a trombonist, arranger, and composer in addition to leading the Russ Morgan Orchestra. "So Tired" (1943), written by Morgan with Jack Stuart, was one of Morgan's better-known compositions.

His most famous song, however, is probably the plaintive, but enduring, number "You're Nobody 'Til Somebody Loves You" (1944), written with Larry Stock and James Cavanaugh. Morgan also collaborated on the moderately well-known "Somebody Else Is Taking My Place" (1937), with Richard Howard and Bob Ellsworth. In addition, Morgan wrote the music for "Does Your Heart Beat for Me?" (1936) to go with the lyrics by Mitchell Parish, another of his themes, as was "So Long (It's Been Good to Know Yuh)" (1935), by Woody Guthrie, Morgan's closing theme. With several good compositions, a number of arrangements, and one of the better big bands, Morgan sustained the Pennsylvania bandleader tradition of accomplishment.

Morgan's associates Stock and Cavanaugh were not exactly loafers either. Stock (1896-) also helped create the following songs: "Blueberry Hill," written in 1940 by Stock, Vincent Rose, and Al Lewis and revived in 1956 by Antoine "Fats" Domino; "The Umbrella Man" (1938), by Stock, Cavanaugh, and Rose; "Did You Ever Get That Feeling in the Moonlight?" (1945), by Cavanaugh, Stock, and Ira Schuster; "The Morning Side of the Mountain" (1951), by Stock and Dick Manning; "Tell Me a Story" (1948), by Maurice Sigler and Stock; and "You Won't Be Satisfied (Until You

Break My Heart)" (1945), by Freddy James and Stock. Cavanaugh (1892-1967) also helped write "Christmas in Killarney" (1950), recorded by Dennis Day and created by Cavanaugh, John Redmond, and Frank Weldon; "The Gaucho Serenade" (1939), by Cavanaugh, Redmond, and Nat Simon; and "I Like Mountain Music" (1933), by Cavanaugh and Redmond.

Big band numbers, rock era songs, Christmas favorites, and even country compositions—quite a diverse output from three busy artists. In spite of the possible implications of another favorite number of the Russ Morgan Orchestra, "Cruising Down the River" (1945, words by Emily Beadell and music by Nell Tollerton), Morgan, Stock, and Cavanaugh didn't seem to take the lazy option in life.

SI ZENTNER
(THE SI ZENTNER ORCHESTRA, 1959-1970s, OCCASIONAL APPEARANCES TO THE PRESENT)

Lazy River

It may be a "Lazy River," but the 1931 composition by Hoagy Carmichael and Sidney Arodin had more than enough energy to make substantial contributions to the careers of two groups of at least moderate reputation. In 1941, the legendary Mills Brothers vocal group made "Lazy River" one of their many hits. Over two decades later, in 1962, the Si Zentner Orchestra recorded "Lazy River" after making it one of their favorite numbers as well as their theme song.

Perhaps the "Lazy River" was not as dormant as it seemed. After all, the opening line, "Up a lazy river," suggests some effort by doing something other than just floating with the current. In addition, its creators, Carmichael (1899-1981), born in Indiana, and Arodin (1901-1948), born in New Orleans, both had active careers. Carmichael was one of the most famous popular composers of the twentieth century, creating the music for two classics, "Stardust" (1927) and "Heart and Soul" (1938). Arodin, although not composing any other notable songs, was a clarinet player of some accomplishment. However, at the same time, Carmichael did tend to write soft and reflective songs, including "Two Sleepy People" (1938), with Frank

Loesser, who also wrote the lyrics for "Heart and Soul," and "Lazy Bones" (1932), with lyricist Johnny Mercer.

Si, or Sy, Zentner (1917-2000), born Simon H. Zentner in Brooklyn, New York, was a trombonist as well as the leader of a successful band. Before he formed his band, he played with Les Brown, Harry James, Jimmy Dorsey, and others. While with James he was featured in the 1942 recording of "Sleepy Lagoon" (1930), music by Eric Coates, lyrics supplied in 1942 by Jack Lawrence. Again the sleepy or lazy motif peeks its head from beneath the covers.

The apparent Zentner preference for slower music continued on one of the several albums on which "Lazy River" appeared, for he also presented "Moon River" (1961), by composer Henry Mancini and lyricist Johnny Mercer. However, some of the other numbers on the same ca. 1963 disc had more musical energy, including the following: the Brazilan composition "Desafinado" ("Slightly Out of Tune") (1962), original Portuguese lyrics by W. Newton Mendonca, English lyrics by Jon Hendricks and Jesse Cavanaugh, music by Antonio Carlos Jobim; "Walk on the Wild Side" (1962), words by Mack David, music by Elmer Bernstein (for the 1962 film of that name); "The Stripper" (1962), music by David Rose (for the 1963 film of the same name); "African Waltz" (1961), words by Mel Mandel and Norman Sachs, music by Galt MacDermot; "From Russia with Love" (1963), words and music by Lionel Bart (for the 1963 film of that name); and "Calcutta" (1960), words by Lee Pockriss and Paul J. Vance, music by Heino Gaze. These songs involved traveling to Brazil, Africa, Russia, and India, plus walking wildly, stripping, waltzing, and going to the movies. Yet Zentner's basic laid-back tendencies again surfaced with another piece on the album, Johnny Smith's 1960 command "Walk—Don't Run."

STAN KENTON
(THE STAN KENTON ORCHESTRA, 1941-1947, 1950-1979)

Artistry in Rhythm

"Artistry in Rhythm" is a good name for a big band number and an appropriate one to describe the work of the Stan Kenton Orchestra. One of the more important big bands, the Kenton ensemble performed a wide variety of works, classical, such as "City of Glass" (1948, by Robert Graettinger), general pops, such as "September Song" (1938, by lyricist Maxwell Anderson and composer Kurt Weill), and jazz, such as "Artistry in Rhythm" (1941, by Stan Kenton [1911-1979]). Depending on the composition chosen and the arranger used, the results of recordings by Kenton have been mixed, but overall he has been influential in American music as a whole and in jazz in particular.

Instrumental "Artistry" was the theme song of the Kenton ensemble and mixed well with arrangements of more conventional popular music. For example, on a 1973 recording, "Artistry" was accompanied by some compositions by standard pops songwriters. One such piece was "Here's That Rainy Day" (1953), by lyricist Johnny Burke (who also wrote the words for the tender standard "Misty" [1955] to go with the melody by Erroll Garner) and musician Jimmy Van Heusen (who wrote a number of top ballads with lyricist Sammy Cahn in the 1950s and 1960s and several other pieces with Burke including Academy Award-winner "Swinging on a Star" [1944]).

Another 1973 nonjazz record mate with "Artistry" was "Invitation" (1952), by lyricist Paul Francis Webster and composer Bronislau Kaper. Similar to "Misty" (which was featured in the 1971 film *Play Misty for Me*) and "Swinging on a Star," the creators of "Invitation" wrote compositions associated with excellent movies. Webster and composer Sammy Fain collaborated on Academy Award-winning "Love Is a Many Splendored Thing" for the 1955 film of that name. Kaper and lyricist Helen Deutsch collaborated on "Hi Lilli, Hi Lo" (1952), sung charmingly by Leslie Caron in the engaging film *Lili*.

Speaking of artistry and rhythm, as in "Artistry in Rhythm," Kenton also very capably recorded George and Ira Gershwin's 1930 "I Got Rhythm" in 1960, as well as another Gershwin classic, the 1926 "Someone to Watch Over Me," in 1963. These recordings further demonstrated the broad versatility of Kenton as a bandleader. Overall, Kenton may have produced an artistically mixed bag, but it was a decades-long container with many good musical prizes.

City of Glass

The senior author's first substantial experience with the music of the Stan Kenton Orchestra was as a college student in the late 1950s. After hearing Kenton's recording of "City of Glass," not once, but three times, to me the name of Kenton was, for a few years, synonymous with weird.

After hearing various other renditions by Kenton, my opinion changed substantially, yet my view of "City of Glass," which I have listened to again in recent years, is only a bit less harsh. Kenton first performed avante-guarde "City" in 1948 and recorded an expanded version in 1951. "City" was a symphonic or classical work created by Robert Graettinger, for a while a close associate of Kenton. Short-lived Graettinger (1923-1957), born in Ontario, California, also wrote "House of Strings" and "Incident in Jazz," both recorded by Kenton in 1950; "This Modern World," recorded around 1951, and "Thermopylae," a 1950s work.

Although performed by a band often associated with jazz, these works by Graettinger were, as a whole, not closely affiliated with the hard-to-define genre of jazz. Yet they, most especially "City of Glass," have been closely associated with versatile and eclectic Kenton, himself somewhat hard to define.

Also hard to define was another Kenton favorite, "Orange-Colored Sky." Musically, that piece was a typical love song and, therefore, not very unusual. (It could be argued, however, that lines such as "Love hit me in the eye," crafted to rhyme with "sky," are not everyday fodder for ballads.) However, conceptually, although a romantic orange-colored sky does sometimes occur at sunset, the context of the song suggests a rare meteorological event. In any case, the 1950 composition by William Stein and Milton DeLugg is a good song, as were some others by DeLugg. With Bob Hilliard, DeLugg also wrote "Be My Life's Companion" (1951), "Sailor Boys Have Talk to Me in English" (1955), and "Shanghai" (1951).

With Sammy Gallop, DeLugg wrote "My Lady Loves to Dance" (1953). With the great Frank Loesser, DeLugg created "Just Another Polka" (1950) and the lively novelty "Hoop-Dee-Doo" (1950), probably his second most successful composition after "Orange." Therefore, the man with the unusual surname is best known for two songs with unusual names that are rarely heard today, and he wrote them both in the same year. In the fickle world of popular music, such short periods of top productivity are far from unusual.

Tampico

Stan Kenton, born Stanley Newcomb Kenton in Wichita, Kansas, was a multitalented musician. Pianist, composer, arranger, and leader of the Stan Kenton Orchestra, he was a major figure in American music from the 1940s until his death. In his role as a pianist, he made many recordings, including his own "Originals for Piano" (1946). In his role as a composer, he created his theme "Artistry in Rhythm" (1941) and was a collaborator on "And Her Tears Flowed Like Wine" (1944), with Joe Greene and Charles Lawrence. In his role as a notable bandleader, he performed many works, including one of his favorites, "Tampico" (1946), words and music by Walter Ruick (who wrote little or nothing else of consequence).

Other compositions recorded by bandleader Kenton also focused on his skill as an arranger. Varying frequently from his most preferred mode, jazz, to which the previous three songs more or less belong, he even provided adaptations for a number of traditional Christmas carols. For a 1961 album, he and Ralph Carmichael wrote unconventional, and often very effective, arrangements for "O Tannenbaum," "The Holly and the Ivy," "We Three Kings of Orient Are," "Good King Wenceslas," "Once in Royal David's City," "God Rest Ye Merry, Gentlemen," "Angels We Have Heard on High," and "O Holy Night." For the same album, Kenton, by himself, reworked "O Come All Ye Faithful," "Joy to the World," "Away in a Manger," "The First Noel," "We Wish You a Merry Christmas," "Hark! The Herald Angels Sing," and "Silent Night."

Perhaps the most striking of these arrangements was the uninhibited rendition of "Good King Wenceslas," one of the more satisfying legacies of good Stan Kenton.

TED HEATH
(THE TED HEATH ORCHESTRA,
1944-1960s)

Listen to My Music

They did listen to his music, and danced to it, on two continents. From 1945 to 1955, Ted Heath (1900-1969) led a highly successful orchestra in Great Britain, and starting in 1955, he also led one of the top swing bands in the United States. He was one of several "Teds" to lead a big band, including Ted Weems, Teddy Wilson, and Ted Lewis, whose theme was "When My Baby Smiles at Me" (1920, words by Lewis and Andrew B. Sterling, music by Bill Munro). During one of their frequent overseas tours, the Ted Heath Orchestra even performed at Carnegie Hall in May 1956, a clear sign that the ensemble compared favorably with America's best.

The recording made on that occasion included Heath's theme, "Listen to My Music," which was created by Heath not long before. The following numbers were also on the disc: "Memories of You" (1930), words by Andy Razaf, music by Eubie Blake; "Perdido" (1942), by Edwin M. Drake, Hans Lengsfelder, and Juan Tizol; "Autumn in New York" (1934), by Vernon Duke; "Carioca" (1933), words by Gus Kahn and Edward Eliscu, music by Vincent Youmans; "Just One of Those Things" (1935), by Cole Porter; "Lullaby in Rhythm" (1938), by Benny Goodman, Edgar Sampson, Clarence Prift, and Walter Hirsch; "I Remember You" (1942), words by Johnny Mercer, music by Victor Schertzinger; and "Hawaiian War

Chant" (1936), words by Ralph Freed, music by John Avery Noble and Leleiohaku. John Noble, incidentally, who also cowrote with Thomas J. Harrison the well-known island song "My Little Grass Shack in Kealakekua, Hawaii" (1933), is not to be confused with bandleader Ray Noble who, like Heath, was born in England.

So Heath not only had the personal qualities to lead the best British swing band, which was a smash in the United States, he also had very good taste in music. No matter how skilled or disciplined an orchestra may be, selection of numbers to perform is an essential key to ultimate success or failure.

That Lovely Weekend

Ted Heath (1900-1969), born in London, England, is remembered as one of the top bandleaders of the middle of the century. He also was a trombone player and to some extent a composer. In 1942, he and his wife Moira created "That Lovely Weekend," the royalties from which helped finance the formation of his band. In the 1950s, he wrote his theme song, "Listen to My Music," which was recorded in 1956.

Ted and Moira have been incorrectly credited with the 1945 composition "I'm Gonna Love That Guy," which was performed by Heath. That song was written by Frances Ash, who is known for nothing else. However, the Ted Heath Orchestra has been correctly credited with very capably performing some of the better songs of the 1940s and 1950s. The following were among the favorite numbers of Heath: the swing classic "Opus One" (1944), by Sy Oliver; the famous "Dragnet" theme (1949), by Walter Schumann; "The Swingin' Shepherd Blues" (1958), words by Rhoda Roberts and Kenny Jacobsen, music by Moe Kossman; and "Hot Toddy" (1953), words by Herb Hendler, music by Ralph Flanagan.

So Heath created a lot of musical heat with his renditions of the dynamic and pulsating "Opus One," the dramatic and tense "Dragnet," the lively "Swingin' Shepherd," and the self-explanatory "Hot Toddy." But it is uncertain whether Heath ever performed the cool and reserved strains of "Serenade," a piece of famous music derived from the 1900 ballet *Les Millions d'Arlequin*, by Italian composer Riccardo Drigo (1846-1930). Hendler, the lyricist for "Hot Toddy," was the handler (with Jerry Gray) of the 1900 melody, providing lyrics to turn it into a swing era number. Yet, as fine a piece of music as is "Serenade," it was perhaps too placid to please the audiences of the time, which were accustomed to the various moods of jazz and the almost endless varieties of dance numbers.

TED WEEMS
(THE TED WEEMS ORCHESTRA,
EARLY 1930s-LATE 1940s)

Heartaches

When the Weems brothers, Ted and Art, formed their own band in 1923, they could have followed the path later chosen by their fellow Pennsylvanians, better-known as the Dorsey brothers. That is, they could have worked together more or less as equals for a while and then split into two somewhat hostile ensembles. However, Ted became the leader of the orchestra not long after its founding and was its maestro for years.

Ted Weems (1901-1963), born in Pitcairn, Pennsylvania, under the name Wilfred Theodore Weymes, was also a trombonist (like his brother) and a composer. Among the songs written by Weems were "The Martins and the Coys" (1936), with Al Cameron, and "Oh Monah" (1931) and "Jig Time" (1931), both with Country Washburn, a singer with the Ted Weems Orchestra. ("The Martins" was later used in the 1946 Walt Disney cartoon *Make Mine Music*, and "Monah" became the theme of bandleader Lew Stone.) Washburn also wrote the lyrics for "One Dozen Roses" (1942), with colyricist Roger Lewis, to go with a melody by Dick Jurgens and Walter Donovan, and Donovan, in turn, cowrote "Aba Daba Honeymoon" (1941, revived in 1951) with Arthur Fields. So Weems's goofy novelty about the feuding hill families, the Martins and the Coys, was artistically connected to the goofy novelty about the honeymoon of a romantic monkey and chimpanzee. It is always interesting to link great works of art.

More substantial than these novelties were Weems's theme, "Out of the Night" (1936), words by Walter Hirsch, music by Harry Sosnick, and the old standard "Heartaches" (1931), a million-selling record by the Ted Weems Orchestra in 1947. The recording, which featured whistler Elmo Tanner, was actually made and released in 1933 but lay dormant for fourteen years. "Heartaches" was the best-known song by John Klenner, who wrote the lyrics while the more successful songwriter Al Hoffman (1902-1960) wrote the melody. Klenner also created "Down the River of Golden Dreams" (1930), with Nathaniel Shilkret; "Just Friends" (1931), words by Sam M. Lewis, music by Klenner; "Smoke Dreams" (1947), with Lloyd Schaefer; and "Whisper That You Love Me" (1942), words by Klenner, music by Hans Engelmann. None of these four were especially popular, turning any golden dreams by Klenner of having another big hit like "Heartaches" into smoke.

Somebody Stole My Gal

One of the biggest hits of the Ted Weems Orchestra was "My Baby Just Cares for Me" (1930), written by the quite successful songwriting team of lyricist Gus Kahn and composer Walter Donaldson. But it seems that "baby" really had romantic interest in others, for one of the favorite numbers of Weems was "Somebody Stole My Gal." Later to be the theme of bandleader Billy Cotton, "Somebody Stole" was created in 1918 by little known songwriter Leo Wood. (We don't know the stolen gal's name, but we know that it wasn't "Nola" [1916, music by Felix Arndt], who hung around the Weems ensemble for quite a while.)

In 1946, Wood also revised a 1924 song by Fred Rose, "Honest and Truly," and helped to write "Runnin' Wild" (1922), words by Joe Grey and Wood, music by A. Harrington Gibbs. Neither of these compositions was particularly famous nor enduring, and none of the persons closely associated with them are particularly notable. However, there are some fascinating historical connections between "Runnin' Wild" and several artists who were notable. That number was inserted into the 1923 musical *Runnin' Wild*, which also included one of the most famous numbers of the twentieth century, "Charleston." Created by Cecil Mack and James (Jimmy) Johnson, "Charleston" became the biggest dance fad in U.S. history. Twenty-three years after its introduction, "Charleston" was featured in the 1946 classic film, *It's a Wonderful Life,* starring noted actors Jimmy Stewart and Donna Reed, directed by Frank Capra.

So Wood's "Somebody Stole My Gal" ran wild for about a generation, directly touching the lives of Weems and Cotton and indirectly snagging the careers of Mack, Johnson, Stewart, Reed, and Capra. Although somebody stole someone else's gal to start it all, the end result was a wonderful life for several persons.

TEDDY WILSON
(THE TEDDY WILSON ORCHESTRA, 1939-1940)

You Can't Stop Me from Dreaming

Theodore Shaw "Teddy" Wilson (1912-1986) is best known as an outstanding jazz pianist who performed with Benny Goodman and others. Yet Wilson, an African American born in Austin, Texas, also did considerable arranging, some composing, and led a first-rate big band for about a year.

Among the numbers preferred by the Teddy Wilson Orchestra were "Carelessly" and "You Can't Stop Me from Dreaming." "Carelessly," a label that could not be applied to the way Wilson approached his music, was written in 1937 by lyricists Charles Kenny (1898-?) and Nick Kenny (1895-1975) and composer Norman Ellis (1899-1974). "You Can't Stop Me from Dreaming," which could well apply to Wilson's artistic outlook, was created in 1937 by Dave (David) Franklin and Cliff Friend. Franklin (1908-1973), born in London, England, and Friend (1893-1974) also collaborated on "When My Dream Boat Comes Home" (1936), a notable song of the time; "Concert in the Park" (1939); "I Must See Annie Tonight" (1938); and "The Merry-Go-Round Broke Down" (1937), the longtime closing theme of Warner Brothers cartoons.

Friend also wrote two other interesting songs with other collaborators. With Carmen Lombardo, the brother of bandleader Guy, he created "The Sweetest Music This Side of Heaven" (1934), a description that could apply to many musicians of the swing era, including Wilson. With Charles Tobias, Friend wrote "We Did It Before (and We Can Do It Again)" (1941). Written on December 7, 1941, the day the Japanese bombed Pearl Harbor, and recorded on December 16, the World War II favorite was a boast that the United States would prevail in war. Unfortunately, it did not apply to Wilson's short-lived big band, which was never revived.

TOMMY DORSEY
(THE TOMMY DORSEY ORCHESTRA, 1935-1953, WITH JIMMY DORSEY AS LEADER 1953-1956)

I'll Never Smile Again

"I'll Never Smile Again" is a strange title for a number that helped bring considerable fame and fortune to the rising vocal star Frank Sinatra. The young man from Hoboken, New Jersey, had come to the attention of a top bandleader, Tommy Dorsey, after his first recording, Jack Lawrence and Arthur Altman's "All or Nothing at All," appeared in 1940. Sinatra had made the disc for another bandleader, Harry James, in 1939, soon after James had discovered Sinatra performing in a New Jersey roadhouse. Although "All or Nothing at All" was not an initial success, Dorsey (1905-1956) recruited the promising singer for his band in 1940, where Sinatra remained until he became very popular and began a solo career in 1942.

Sinatra's first recording with Dorsey was Ruth C. Lowe's "I'll Never Smile Again" (1940). It was a top seller and became one of Sinatra's standards. Sinatra performed the ballad with the Dorsey Orchestra again in 1941 for the film *Las Vegas Nights*. Sinatra also collaborated with Dorsey on the vocalist's first million-selling record, "There Are Such Things" (1941), words by Abel Baer and Stanley Adams and music by George W. Meyer.

Lowe (1920-1985), the creator of "I'll Never Smile Again," only wrote one more song of consequence, "Put Your Dreams Away for Another Day" (1942), a theme of Sinatra, writing the lyrics to go with Paul Mann and Stephan Weiss's melody. Dorsey, however, had many other hits, becoming one of the elite of swing era bandleaders. The following were among the other successful recordings by the Dorsey ensemble: "Stardust," words by Mitchell Parish (1929), music by Hoagy Carmichael (1927); "On the Sunny Side of the Street" (1930), words by Dorothy Fields, music by Jimmy McHugh; "Day In—Day Out" (1939), by Johnny Mercer and Rube Bloom; "Royal Garden Blues" (1919), music by Clarence Williams and Spencer Williams; "Song of India," music derived from Nikolay Rimsky-Korsakov's *Sheherazade* (1888); "Who" (1925), words by Oscar Hammerstein II and Otto Harbach, music by Jerome Kern; "Indian Summer," music by Victor Herbert (1919), words by Al Dubin (1940); "Dolores" (1941), words by Frank Loesser, music by Louis Alter; and "Once in a While" (1937), words by Bud Green, music by Michael Edwards. In other words, Dorsey recorded hit songs more than once in a while.

I'm Getting Sentimental Over You

In the 1947 film tribute to the feuding, but very talented, Dorsey brothers, *The Fabulous Dorseys,* several fine songs associated with either Tommy or Jimmy were performed. However, possibly deliberately, none of the theme songs of either bandleader were part of the movie's score. Perhaps as a concession to the brothers who had split into two separate bands in 1935, Jimmy's "Contrasts" (1941, music by Jimmy), Tommy's "Opus One" (1944, music by Sy Oliver), and Tommy's "I'm Getting Sentimental Over You" (1933, words by Ned Washington, music by George Bassman), were absent from the film. Unfortunately, in addition to a partial distortion of history by these exclusions, the film's audience was not able to hear the strains of these three very good pieces.

"I'm Getting Sentimental," a fine slow tempo ballad, was the first signature song of the Tommy Dorsey Orchestra and also the first big hit of outstanding lyricist Ned Washington (1901-1976). Among the other notable songs on which Washington collaborated were the following: "The Nearness of You" (1940), with composer Hoagy Carmichael; "My Foolish Heart" (1949), with composer Victor Young; "When You Wish Upon a Star," for the 1940 Disney animated classic *Pinocchio,* with composer Leigh Harline (the piece would become Disney's musical theme); and the themes for the films *High Noon* (1952) and *The High and The Mighty* (1954), plus the theme for the television series *Rawhide* (1959-1966), all three with composer Dmitri Tiomkin.

Washington's creation of the lyrics for these songs gave him direct or indirect connections with several top entertainment celebrities of the middle third of the twentieth century. Celebrated composers Carmichael, Young, and Tiomkin; cartoon genius Walt Disney; film stars Gary Cooper and Grace Kelly (*High Noon*); film legend John Wayne (*The High and the Mighty*); eventual Hollywood legend Clint Eastwood (*Rawhide*); and, not least of all, swing era legend Tommy Dorsey—all had some artistic debt to wordsmith Washington. In turn, of course, much of the world in the 1930s, 1940s, and 1950s had substantial artistic and sentimental debts to the great bandleader Dorsey.

Marie

The two Dorsey Brothers, Tommy and Jimmy, and the five Marx Brothers, Groucho, Chico, Harpo and sometimes Gummo and Zeppo, had various associations with movies. For example, two of Tommy Dorsey's favorite numbers, "Marie" and "Alone," performed by others, appeared in films. "Marie," words and music by Irving Berlin, premiered in the 1928 film *The Awakening,* and "Alone," words by Arthur Freed, music by Nacio Herb Brown, premiered in the 1935 film *A Night at the Opera.* The real stars of the 1935 production, of course, were the Marx Brothers, with Groucho, Chico, and Harpo bringing delightful chaos to the opera house. (Incidently, Tommy is reputed to have been as much of a character in real life as were any of the Marx Brothers in their act.) Another song first appearing in the latter movie, "Cosi Cosa," words by Ned Washington, music by Bronislau Kaper and Walter Jurmann, also was overshadowed by the antics of the three clownish siblings.

Tommy and Jimmy were in one sense alone after the dissolution of the Dorsey Brothers Orchestra in 1935. (Possibly, Tommy was predicting the future of the brothers when he wrote "Givin' Me Blues," which was recorded in 1928.) However, Freed and Brown, similar to the Marx Brothers, worked together successfully for some time. Lyricist Freed (1894-1973) and composer Brown (1896-1964) collaborated on "You Were Meant for Me" (1929), "Singin' in the Rain" (1929), "Temptation" (1933), "All I Do Is Dream of You" (1934), "My Lucky Star" (1935), and "Make 'em Laugh" (1952).

Freed and Brown's "Alone" and, even more, Berlin's expansive "Marie" were standards in Dorsey's repertory. The latter composition, recorded by the Dorsey ensemble in January 1937 with vocalist Jack Leonard, was one of the favorites of the swing era, along with the orchestra that helped make the piece famous.

Opus One

With a title (or nontitle) such as "Opus One," you might expect that the work was indeed the first created by its composer. However, though Sy (Melvin James) Oliver did not write a lot of songs, his 1944 swing classic was not his first composition. Oliver (1910-1988) also wrote "Yes Indeed" (1941), which, similar to "Opus One," was recorded by the Tommy Dorsey Orchestra, and the music of "For Dancers Only" (1937), a favorite of Jimmie Lunceford. Yet in a sense "Opus One," a very lively and dynamic instrumental with a dominating beat, was properly named. Later used by Dick Clark in his television music show *American Bandstand,* "Opus One" was by far the finest achievement of Oliver and one of the very best numbers of the swing era. It also became one of Dorsey's signature songs.

Two other outstanding songs affiliated with Dorsey were the jazz classic "Boogie Woogie" (1928), music by short-lived Clarence "Pine Top" Smith (1904-1929), who died from an accidental shooting in a Chicago dance hall, and the very danceable and near classic "Little White Lies" (1930), words and music by Walter Donaldson, recorded by Dorsey in 1937. "Boogie Woogie," recorded by Dorsey in 1938, reportedly sold four million records. Both of these pieces still were heard with some regularity in the 1990s.

Donaldson (1893-1947) also contributed the music for a 1936 song, "You (Gee But You're Wonderful)," to the Dorsey repertory. That piece was written with lyricist Harold Adamson. Composer Donaldson also helped create a number of other memorable songs, including the Benny Goodman hit "Love Me or Leave Me" (1928), "Yes Sir, That's My Baby" (1925), "Makin' Whoopee" (1928), and "My Baby Just Cares for Me" (1930), all four with noted lyricist Gus Kahn. In fact, in contrast to Sy Oliver, Donaldson was a major supplier of good material to the big bands, and that is not a little white lie.

WILL BRADLEY
(THE WILL BRADLEY ORCHESTRA, 1939-1942)

Beat Me Daddy, Eight to the Bar

If you view the title of "Beat Me Daddy, Eight to the Bar" in any context other than music, the connotations are quite negative. However, in its real context, a fast-paced, strong rhythm jazz number, the results are very positive. One of the favorite pieces of the Will Bradley Orchestra, "Beat Me" helped trombonist Bradley become a significant bandleader in the swing era. Bradley (1912-   ), born Wilbur Schwichtenberg in Newton, New Jersey, also did some composing, including one of the band's themes, "Strange Cargo," created in the late 1930s; another theme, "Think of Me" (1941), with Carl Sigman and Freddie Slack; and several classical works. "Strange Cargo" was to become the theme of the Freddie Slack Orchestra.

One of the composers of "Beat Me" (1940, words and music by Hughie Prince, Don Raye, and Eleanor Sheehy) also helped write a classic in another genre. Totally different from the hip "Beat Me," although written in the same year, was the reflective and smooth patriotic standard "This Is My Country" (1940), words by the aforementioned Raye, music by Al Jacobs. However, except for this exceptional tribute to America, Raye's compositions were all directed toward the popular domain. Raye (1909-1985) and Prince also collaborated on "Boogie Woogie Bugle Boy (from Company

B)" (1941), a World War II era favorite, and "Rum Boogie" (or "Rhumboogie") (1940). Prince, who seemed to favor songs with interesting titles, also created "I Guess I'll Get the Papers and Go Home" (1946), with Dick Rogers and Hal Kanner.

Raye also leaned toward that type of title with other collaborators. With Gene DePaul, he wrote "Milkman, Keep Those Bottles Quiet" (1944) and "Cow-Cow Boogie" (1942), the latter also with Benny Carter. (Note the milk connection of these two numbers.) "Cow-Cow Boogie" may be a reference to Charles "Cow-Cow" Davenport, who wrote the jazz classic "(I'll Be Glad When You're Dead) You Rascal You" (1931) plus a lesser work, "Mama Don't Allow No Easy Riders Here" (1929). Perhaps wishing to demonstrate that they could produce nonmilky compositions with conventional titles, Raye and DePaul also created "He's My Guy" (1942); "I'll Remember April" (1942), with Patricia Johnston; "Irresistible You" (1944); "Lovely Luana" (1945); and "Star Eyes" (1943). However, away from Prince and DePaul, Raye often strayed toward the unusual with pieces such as "The House of Blue Lights" (1947), with Freddie Slack; "They Were Doing the Mambo" (1954), with Sonny Burke; and "Scrub Me Mama with a Boogie Beat" (1940), by himself. "Scrub Me," a companion boogie-woogie style curiosity to "Beat Me," was also a hit for the Bradley band.

A whole generation before the offbeat Mamas and the Papas were a late-1960s rock vocal group, Bradley had an orchestral group with its own kind of mama and papa, ones with a strong jazz beat.

High on a Windy Hill

Trombonist Will Bradley created a lot of musical wind, as did the rest of the Will Bradley Orchestra during its time as a popular ensemble. So having a favorite number with a title such as "High on a Windy Hill" probably was appropriate for this or any big band. Written in 1941 by Alex C. Kramer and Joan Whitney, "Windy Hill" was just one of several good compositions by the pair. It also was a number-one hit for Jimmy Dorsey that year.

Kramer (1903-1998) and Whitney (1914-1990) also collaborated on the following numbers: "Candy" (1944) and "It's Love, Love, Love" (1944), both with Mack David; "It All Comes Back to Me Now" (1941), "My Sister and I" (1941), and "No Other Arms, No Other Lips" (1959), all three with Hy Zaret; "Comme Ci, Comme Ça" (1949), with Bruno Coquatrix and Pierre Dudan; "Love Somebody" (1944), "Far Away Places" (1949), "That's the Beginning of the End" (1946), and "The Way the Wind Blows" (1946), all four with no outside help. Whitney and Zaret also worked together on "So You're the One" (1941).

The previous set of songs is quite interesting from a historical viewpoint. "Windy Hill" did not have sufficient artistic force to keep the Bradley band together for very long, for it broke up in 1942. Yet succulent "Candy" and the romantic Doris Day standard "Love Somebody" have been enduring, and dreamy "Far Away Places" can still be heard occasionally. The arena of popular music is tricky and fickle, or, to put it from the perspective of underappreciated Kramer and Whitney, that's the way the wind blows.

Other songs favored or recorded by the Bradley ensemble have also been mostly blown away by the perfidious winds of the years. These include a batch of compositions recorded in 1939 to 1941: "Jimtown Blues" (1942), words and music by Fred Rose; "Deed I Do" (1927), words by Walter Hirsch, music by Rose; "Memphis Blues" (1912), words by George A. Norton, music by W. C. Handy;

"In a Little Spanish Town" (1926), words by Sam M. Lewis and Joe Young, music by Mabel Wayne; "The Five O'Clock Whistle" (1940), words and music by Kim Gannon, William C. K. Irwin, and Josef Myrow (also known as Joseph Myrow); "I'm Coming, Virginia" (1926), words and music by Will Marion Cook and Donald Heywood; "Hallelujah" (1927), words by Clifford Grey and Leo Robin, music by Vincent Youmans; "I Don't Stand a Ghost of a Chance with You" (1932), words by Bing Crosby and Ned Washington, music by Victor Young; "After I Say I'm Sorry" (1926), words and music by Walter Donaldson and Abe Lyman; and "Celery Stalks at Midnight" (1940), words and music by Carl Sigman. Although some of these pieces had some degree of fame, for example, "Memphis Blues," "In a Little Spanish Town," and "Hallelujah," most of them (plus other less identifiable numbers in the Bradley repertory) are just obscurities in the history of American popular music. The title of the song about the night-stalking vegetable, however, deserves to be preserved as a prime example of how language can be twisted to mean just about anything.

WOODY HERMAN
(THE WOODY HERMAN
ORCHESTRA, 1936-1987)

Caledonia

During the 1940s, there were a fair amount of parades in the United States. In large part, this was due to World War II and its aftermath, including inevitable victory parades with their also-inevitable military and patriotic songs. However, some parades were also associated with popular music. In 1940, the enduring composition "South Rampart Street Parade" was created by Ray Bauduc, Robert Haggart, and later famous comedian Steve Allen. In 1943, the film *Youth on Parade* included "(It Seems to Me) I've Heard That Song Before," written by lyricist Sammy Cahn and musician Jule Styne.

Another film, *Swing Parade of 1946*, presented "Caledonia (What Makes Your Head So Hard)." Written by obscure Fleecie Moore in 1946, "Caledonia" became one of the favorites of the Woody Herman Orchestra. Woodrow Charles Herman (1913-1987), born in Milwaukee, was a singer, alto sax player, and clarinet player but is best known as a bandleader of considerable importance. (A less famous bandleader named Herman was Lenny Herman. The theme of the Lenny Herman Orchestra was "No Foolin'" [1926], words by Gene Buck, music by James M. Hanley.) During the 1930s, Woody's ensemble was described as "the band that plays the blues" (although his repertory was much wider than that). At other times, for example, when Herman made a hit 1946 recording of "The Good Earth" (1944), an instrumental by Neal Hefti, the group was called "Woody Herman and the Herd." (Hefti with Herman wrote another instrumental hit for Herman, "Wild Root" [1946]).

Among the numbers that helped to sustain Herman's reputation as the leader of a top jazz group was the classic blues piece "Blues in the Night." Created in 1941 by two famous songwriters, lyricist Johnny Mercer and composer Harold Arlen, "Blues" was a mainstay for Herman's band and other ensembles of the period. Written for a film that originally had the title *Hot Nocturne,* the initial impact of the composition caused a fast change in film title to match the song's very colorful (in more than one sense) title. Although hard-headed Caledonia brought on the blues in 1946, Herman's ensemble had the blues for a half decade before.

Early Autumn

The arrival of autumn is, among other things, noted by a predominant shift of winds from the south and the west to winds from the northwest and north. It was, perhaps, just an unconscious fluke that one of Woody Herman's top numbers, "Northwest Passage" (1945), preceded by a few years another top Herman number, "Early Autumn" (1949). But with artists and their complex creative processes, one can never know for sure the true origins of artistic choices and decisions.

"Northwest Passage" was the combined creation of Greig Stewart Jackson, Herman, and Ralph Burns. Both an arranger and band member with the Woody Herman Orchestra, Burns (1922-) also collaborated with Herman (1913-1987) on the music for the later (and possibly subliminally related) "Early Autumn." The lyricist for the 1949 number was the great Johnny Mercer (1909-1976), who also wrote the lyrics for another Herman favorite, "Blues in the Night" (1941), with Harold Arlen writing the music.

Mercer collaborated on, or wrote himself, so many famous songs that a list of them would be overwhelming. His lesser-known songs include "You Have Taken My Heart" (1933), words by Mercer, music by Gordon Jenkins; "When a Woman Loves a Man" (1938), words and music by Mercer, Jenkins, and Bernard Hanighan; and "P.S., I Love You" (1934), words by Mercer, music by Jenkins. The latter song is not to be confused with a 1962 hit of the same title by The Beatles, written by John Lennon and Paul McCartney. Neither "P.S." song could possibly be confused with the hilarious "Strip Polka" (1942), written by Mercer alone and delightfully rendered by the Andrews Sisters, who could not possibly be confused with the Liverpool lads. And "Strip Polka," which involves the indoor activities of a burlesque theater, is totally unaffected by whatever direction the wind may be blowing or whatever season it may be.

Woodchopper's Ball

It is hard to picture what may occur at a woodchopper's ball, if you take this title literally. But if you look at the title figuratively, because of its close association with bandleader "Woody" Herman and the lively tempo of the composition ("chopping" and "having a ball"), it all makes sense from an artistic perspective. Written by Herman and his associate Joe Bishop in 1939, "Woodchopper's Ball," a fast blues number, was the biggest hit of the Woody Herman Orchestra. Little-known Bishop was one of the more important members of Herman's ensemble, playing the flugelhorn and doing some arranging.

Although "Woodchopper's" sold a million records, nothing else by either composer was as successful. For example, Bishop was only involved with the creation of two other notable pieces: "Blue Prelude" (1933), words by Bishop, melody by Gordon Jenkins, and "Blue Flame" (1942), words by Leo Corday, music by Jimmy Noble and Bishop. Both of these "blue" songs were themes of Herman.

The aforementioned Jenkins, however, created several good songs of the 1930s, 1940s, and 1950s. Among these were "Goodbye" (1936), the closing theme of the Benny Goodman Orchestra; "San Fernando Valley" (1944); "Homesick—That's All" (1945); "Tzena, Tzena, Tzena" (1950), words by Jenkins, music arranged by Spencer Ross from a Yiddish folksong; "Married I Can Always Get" (1956); and "This Is All I Ask" (1958).

Incidentally, as unlikely as it may seem, there was more than one version of "Tzena, Tzena, Tzena." There was, however, only one true version of "Woodchopper's Ball," the symbol of one of the more influential big bands of the 1930s and 1940s. "Woodchopper's" was born with Woody Herman and, to a large extent, also died with him.

THE SWEET BANDS

BEN BERNIE
(THE BEN BERNIE ORCHESTRA, 1920s–MID-1930s)

Au Revoir, Pleasant Dreams

"Au Revoir, Pleasant Dreams" was the sign-off theme of bandleader Ben Bernie (1891-1943). (His opening theme was "It's a Lonesome Old Town," or "Lonesome Old Town" (1930), by Harry Tobias and Charles Kisco, which also was the theme of the Jimmy Palmer Orchestra.)

"Au Revoir" was also sung (or, more accurately, spoken) by Bernie, with his deep, resonant voice and his trademark expression "Yassuh, Yassuh, Yassuh." Written by Jack Meskill (lyrics) and Jean Schwartz (music) in 1930 and recorded by Bernie in 1941, it was the trademark of the Ben Bernie Orchestra. Meskill also created "(It Happened) on the Beach at Bali Bali" (1936), words and music by Meskill, Al Sherman, and Abner Silver; "Rhythm of the Rain" (1935), words and music by Meskill and Jack Stern; "There's Danger in Your Eyes, Cherie" (1929), words and music by Meskill, Harry Richman, and Peter Wendling; and "Wonderful You" (1929), words by Meskill and Max Rich, music by Wendling.

Perhaps the oddest song by Meskill was the aforementioned "Bali Bali." (Whether "Bali Bali" has any relationship to the island of Bali in Indonesia is uncertain, but choosing a name that might be associated with a real place famous for its music and dancing is ideal for a dance orchestra.) Possibly, the unconventional nature of "Bali Bali" is in part due to the creative presence of Al Sherman, who collaborated on two other popular curiosities of the 1930s. In 1931, Sherman and Al Lewis wrote the Eddie Cantor hit "(Potatoes Are Cheaper—Tomatoes Are Cheaper) Now's the Time to Fall in Love," and in 1933, Sherman, Lewis, and Buddy Fields produced the enduring sports rouser "You Gotta Be a Football Hero (to Get Along with the Beautiful Girls)."

Meskill's collaborator Jean Schwartz (1878-1956), in contrast to these lively pieces, wrote another number more in line with the sleep theme of Bernie's "Au Revoir." In 1918, Schwartz wrote the music for "Rockabye Your Baby with a Dixie Melody" to accompany the lyrics of Joe Young and Sam M. Lewis. The combination of "Dixie Melody," "Au Revoir," and Bernie's soothing tones are a good recipe for a restful night, along with an evening of dancing to Bernie's band or any others of the swing era.

Sweet Georgia Brown

"Sweet Georgia Brown," the lively jazz classic long associated with the Harlem Globetrotters basketball team, was also long associated with bandleader Ben Bernie. Bernie, Maceo Pinkard, and Kenneth Casey are credited with the composition of the enduring 1925 winner. However, there have been claims that Bernie was not a collaborator on the piece, although his name is usually given first in the credits and Bernie was a primary propagator of the number.

Whether Bernie, who was born in Bayonne, New Jersey, under the name of Benjamin Anzelwitz, helped to write this renowned song may never be clearly proven either way. However, he clearly was a more than competent musician and a pleasant entertainment personality. He did write another song, "Strange Interlude" (1932), words by Bernie and Walter Hirsch, music by Phil Baker. (Hirsch also wrote "Lullaby in Rhythm" [1938], with Benny Goodman, Edgar Sampson, and Clarence Prift.) If Bernie was not a cocreator of "Georgia Brown," Pinkard was most likely the driving force behind the song. Pinkard does have two other significant song credits: "Sugar" (1927), with Sidney D. Mitchell, and "Gimme a Little Kiss, Will Ya, Huh?" (1926), words by Roy Turk and Jack Smith, music by Pinkard. (Turk also wrote the words for "Into My Heart" [1930], music by Fred E. Ahlert, the theme of the Jack Russell Orchestra.) No matter what the complete truth about the legendary 1925 song may be, Ben Bernie and "Georgia Brown" were artistic partners for a long time.

Also long musical associates of the Ben Bernie Orchestra were the buddy in "My Buddy" and the sweet gal in "Ain't She Sweet?". "My Buddy" was created in 1922 by lyricist Gus Kahn and composer Walter Donaldson, and "Ain't She Sweet" was created in 1927 by lyricist Jack Yellen and composer Milton Ager. Both pieces were among the favorite numbers of Bernie. But with the supposed deception and duplicity in the matter of "Georgia Brown," it is fortunate that the buddy and the sweet gal didn't sneak around behind Bernie's back and abandon him altogether.

DICK JURGENS
(THE DICK JURGENS ORCHESTRA,
1928-1955)

Careless

The word "moderate" jumps out when the career of bandleader Dick Jurgens is reviewed. Born in the moderate-sized city of Sacramento, California, Jurgens (1911-) was a musician of apparently moderate ambitions, gravitating toward being a hotel and ballroom bandleader. In the 1930s, the Dick Jurgens Orchestra, including Jurgens' brother Will, was a resident ensemble at the Avalon Ballroom on Catalina Island in California, the Elitch Gardens in Denver, and the Aragon Ballroom in Chicago. After Dick and Will served in World War II as entertainers in the South Pacific, the orchestra returned to the Aragon plus another Chicago ballroom, the Trianon, until 1956. After a thirteen-year absence from the music business, Dick formed another band for another club near Chicago until he retired in 1976.

Jurgens' orchestras were of moderate importance, and Jurgens, himself, was only moderately dedicated to the pursuit of music. Even his orchestra had a moderate style somewhat between the hot sounds of the swing orchestras and other jazz ensembles and the saccharine sounds of the ultrasweet bands, such as those of Guy Lombardo and Jan Garber. Although the Jurgens group had a relatively soft, polished, and texturally rich style that would definitely categorize them as a sweet band, they were possibly closer in philosophy to the softer swing bands, such as the Glenn Miller Orchestra, than to the fuzzy, but pleasant, Lombardo.

The Jurgens Orchestra, in addition, only had moderately successful hits, such as "Careless," "Elmer's Tune," "One Dozen Roses," "A Million Dreams Ago," and "If I Knew Then (What I Know Now)." None of them sold a million records. All of these numbers were created by Jurgens with various collaborators, making Jurgens a songwriter of modest accomplishment. "Careless" (1940), perhaps Jurgens' favorite, was written with Lew Quadling and Eddy Howard, who was a vocalist and guitarist with Jurgens. "Elmer's Tune" (1941), written with Elmer Albrecht and Sammy Gallop, was another top favorite, though possibly more associated with Glenn Miller, who turned it into a standard of his seemingly everlasting repertory. "One Dozen Roses" (1942) was by lyricists Roger Lewis and Country Washburn and composers Walter Donovan and Jurgens. "A Million Dreams Ago" (1940) was written with Quadling and Howard. "If I Knew Then" (1939) was written with Howard. (Later on, Howard formed his own Eddy Howard Orchestra and adopted "Careless," "A Million Dreams," "If I Knew," and another piece entirely by him, "My Last Goodbye" (1939), as his themes.)

Jurgens also wrote his own theme song, "Day Dreams Come True at Night" (1940), not a well-known piece, and another obscurity, "I Won't Be Home Anymore When You Call" (1947), written with Billy Fairmann. Also not especially well known was a number introduced and featured by the Jurgens Orchestra, but not created by him, "Goodnight Mother" (1940). Mack David, Al Bryan, and Vee Lawnhurst collaborated on "Mother." Jurgens was not a national music headliner, as were some other bandleaders, but he was a fixture, particularly in California and Illinois, for a number of years.

EDDY DUCHIN
(THE EDDY DUCHIN ORCHESTRA, 1931-EARLY 1940s, 1946-1950)

I Won't Dance

The Eddy Duchin Orchestra was one of the more successful bands of the 1930s and 1940s, primarily catering to the tastes of the upper crust of American society in live, radio, and film appearances. As a whole, they stayed away from jazz numbers and tended to prefer more conventional and mainstream music. Among their favorite compositions were "I Won't Dance," "Let's Fall in Love," and "Moon Over Miami."

"I Won't Dance" (1935), a somewhat comedic yet stylish number, has a fine musical pedigree. The lyrics were by the notable lyricist Otto Harbach (1873-1963) and the great lyricist Oscar Hammerstein II (1895-1960), and the music was by the outstanding composer Jerome Kern (1885-1945). The song was added to the 1935 movie version of the top 1933 Broadway musical *Roberta*, which featured the sophisticated classic "Smoke Gets in Your Eyes." Also inserted in the film was another fine standard, "Lovely to Look At," lyrics by one of the best male-female songwriting teams, Jimmy McHugh and Dorothy Fields, music by Kern. Fields and Kern collaborated on another romantic gem, "The Way You Look Tonight" (1936), and Fields wrote the lyrics for yet another winner, "I'm in the Mood for Love" (1935), to accompany the melody by McHugh.

The breezy "Let's Fall in Love" (1933) was created by lyricist Ted Koehler and top popular composer Harold Arlen, who also collaborated on the classic "Stormy Weather" in the same year. "Moon Over Miami" (1935) was by two far-from-famous songwriters, lyricist Edgar Leslie and composer Joseph A. Burke. (Leslie also wrote the words for "Romance" [1929], the theme of the Ray Herbeck Orchestra, with better-known composer Walter Donaldson.) "Moon" was a sophisticated ballad and described a romantic occasion in a favorite resort area. All three numbers, in addition, were quite appropriate pieces for Duchin's polished piano artistry. "I Won't Dance," particularly, was an almost ideal choice for the Duchin band, which was perhaps designed more for listening to at supper clubs than for dancing.

My Twilight Dream

It is quite fitting that Eddy Duchin (1909-1951), an excellent pianist with a smooth, suave, sophisticated style, chose as his theme a song based on the music of another fine, but short-lived, pianist, Polish-French classical composer Frédéric Chopin (1810-1849). It is also a bit eerie that the two were born almost exactly one century apart and died close to one century apart. Furthermore, both were honored by biographical films, a common event for top classical composers, but less common for moderately famous popular artists. In Duchin's case, the film was *The Eddy Duchin Story* (1956), starring handsome Tyrone Power.

Duchin, born in Cambridge, Massachusetts, played piano for the notable Leo Reisman Orchestra in the late 1920s and formed the Eddy Duchin Orchestra in 1931. The theme of that mostly swanky, high-society ensemble was "My Twilight Dream" (1939), written by Duchin and vocalist Lew Sherwood, based on Chopin's Nocturne in E-flat (1843). (Duchin's "Twilight" and Chopin's Nocturne also blend together conceptually.) The romance aspired for in that 1939 number seemed to have been satisfied by another Duchin favorite, "Three O'Clock in the Morning" (1921), words by Dorothy Terriss, music by Julian Robledo.

Less glittering and romantic than the Polish and polish of the aforementioned persons, bands, and music was Duchin's 1938 recording of "Ol' Man Mose" (1938). On one of the occasions that the Duchin band varied from their normal sophisticated and sweet repertory to perform a hotter jazz number, the result was embarrassing. The word "bucket" was mispronounced as a vulgar term several times, resulting in the recording being banned in some places. "Ol' Man Mose" was written by the jazz great Louis Armstrong and Zilner Trenton Rudolph. (The theme songs of the Louis Armstrong Orchestra, incidentally, were "Sleepy Time Down South," or "When It's Sleepy Time Down South" [1931], by Leon Rene, Otis

Rene, and Clarence Muse, and "On the Sunny Side of the Street'
[1930], words by Dorothy Fields, music by Jimmy McHugh.)

Other pieces by Armstrong not known to be recorded by Duchin
were "Brother Bill" (1942); "Wild Man Blues" (1927), by Armstrong and Ferdinand Joseph Morton; and a piece with a most
interesting title, "Struttin' with Some Barbecue" (1927), by Armstrong and Lil Hardin. It is understandable why Duchin chose not to
record "Barbecue," presuming he knew about it. Could you imagine
a polite, upper-class supper club audience having anything to do
with hot barbecue sauce, whether literally eaten or figuratively
strutted to, during the 1930s or 1940s?

Despite Duchin's problems with "Ol' Man Mose," it was one of
the numbers included in a 1976 reissue of various numbers recorded by the Duchin ensemble from 1932 to 1938. Others on the
reissue included "By the Fireside" (1932), by Ray Noble, James
Campbell, and Reginald Connelly; "Between the Devil and the
Deep Blue Sea" (1931), words by Ted Koehler, music by Harold
Arlen; and "Try a Little Tenderness" (1932), by Campbell, Connelly, and Harry Woods.

FREDDY MARTIN
(THE FREDDY MARTIN
ORCHESTRA, 1929-1960s)

I've Got a Lovely Bunch
of Cocoanuts

Perhaps best known as television's "Merry Mailman" of the 1950s, Fred Heatherton (1910?-   ) was a bandleader, singer, and composer, though not highly successful at any of these activities. Heatherton wrote only one song of note, the delightful and memorable 1948 novelty "I've Got a Lovely Bunch of Cocoanuts." With three beats and vocal emphasis given to the word "lovely," "Cocoanuts" was a big hit in the late 1940s for the Freddy Martin Orchestra. Curiously, one of the other preferred numbers of the Martin ensemble, and additional compositions by its creators, also had some kind of association with the tropics.

In addition to the previous "cocoanut" connection, there was a trip to tropical Central America with "Managua, Nicaragua" (1947), a Martin favorite, words by Albert Gamse, music by Irving Fields. Lyricist Gamse and composer Fields also took audiences to semi-tropical South Florida with their 1946 "Miami Beach Rhumba" (original Spanish lyrics by Johnnie Camacho). Gamse and Fields, in addition, perhaps suggested the warm French islands of the Caribbean with their 1957 "Chantez, Chantez." Latin America was clearly the venue of "Amapola," or "Pretty Little Poppy" (1924), for which Gamse wrote a set of English lyrics. Joseph M. Lacalle wrote the original Spanish lyrics, an English translation, and the melody for "Amapola," which was a top number of the Jimmy Dorsey Orchestra.

As far as is known, however, Martin (1906-1983) had no particular association with the other famous edible product from tropical trees, bananas. The 1957 calypso hit "The Banana Boat Song," or "Day-O," by Erik Darling, Bob Carey, and Alan Arkin, and the 1923 visit to the fruit stand "Yes, We Have No Bananas," by Frank Silver and Irving Cohn, were not part of the everyday repertory of the Freddy Martin bunch.

Tonight We Love

What do Isham Jones and Freddy Martin have in common in addition to being born in Ohio and being leaders of successful sweet bands? Although there might be a number of valid responses to this inquiry, one particular connection seems to stand out. Both Jones and Martin recorded adaptations of the theme from the first movement of Peter Ilich Tchaikovsky's world-famous Piano Concerto No. 1 (1875). The Isham Jones Orchestra performed "There Is No Greater Love" (1936), words by Marty Symes, music adapted from Tchaikovsky (1840-1893) by Jones. The Freddy Martin Orchestra performed Martin's arrangement of the theme in the 1930s and produced a top hit in 1941 with "Tonight We Love," music adapted by Ray Austin and Martin, words by Bobby Worth. "Tonight" became Martin's number-one theme.

Martin, Austin, and Worth tried another borrowing from the masters in 1942, this time from the Concerto in A Minor for Piano and Orchestra (1868) by Norwegian composer Edvard Grieg (1843-1907). "I Look at Heaven," however, was not nearly as successful. Also not particularly popular with the public was another of Martin's themes, "Early in the Mornin'" (1947), by Leo Hickman, Louis Jordan, and Dallas Bartley.

Martin, born in Cleveland, Ohio, played drums early and tenor saxophone later. In 1931, Martin formed his own band with a smooth, sweet, syrupy style following the model of Guy Lombardo and his Royal Canadians and very successfully performed for about a half century in hotels, on radio and television, and in films. Never varying his musical outlook, despite being the music director for Elvis Presley's first Las Vegas appearance, he led his ensemble almost to his death. He produced dreamy music, had a dream career, and had the famous song "Dream" (1944), by the famous songwriter Johnny Mercer, as a favorite number.

GUY LOMBARDO
(GUY LOMBARDO
AND HIS ROYAL CANADIANS,
1922-1971)

Boo-Hoo

In the nineteenth century, the name "Carmen" associated with classical music referred to the great 1875 French opera of that name by composer Georges Bizet. In the twentieth century, the name "Carmen" associated with American popular music usually referred to Carmen Lombardo (1902-1971), the brother of legendary bandleader Guy Lombardo (1902-1977) and a composer of consequence. (Two other brothers, Lebert and Victor, also worked with Guy.) One of the latter-day Carmen's best-known songs was "Boo-Hoo" (1937), written with Edward Heyman and John Jacob Loeb. A light and lively number with mock tears, "Boo-Hoo" was a favorite of Guy Lombardo and his Royal Canadians. In contrast, the earlier *Carmen* was a not so light, but still lively, favorite with plenty of real tears.

The twentieth-century Carmen and Loeb collaborated on other songs played by brother Guy, including "Get Out Those Old Records" (1951), which was still heard in the 1990s on nostalgia programs; "Seems Like Old Times" (1945), the longtime theme song of radio and television personality Arthur Godfrey; and "Sailboat in the Moonlight" (1937). Carmen also wrote the following numbers: "The Sweetest Music This Side of Heaven" (1934), the theme song of bandleader Maurice Winnick, with Cliff Friend; the music for "Sweethearts on Parade" (1928) lyrics by Charles Newman; "Powder Your Face with Sunshine" (1949), with Stanley Rochinski; "Coquette" (1928), one of Guy's themes, with cocomposer John W. Green and lyricist Gus Kahn; the music for "Return to Me" (1958), lyrics by Danny Di Minno; and the music for "Snuggled on Your Shoulder, Cuddled in Your Arms" (1932), lyrics by Joe Young. Carmen's collaborator Loeb also wrote the music for "Reflections in the Water" (1933) and "Masquerade" (1932), to go with lyrics by Paul Francis Webster; the music for "Got the Jitters" (1934), to go with lyrics by Webster and Billy Rose; and "Sweetie Pie" (1934), by himself.

Some of Carmen's songs are very appropriate descriptions of the music played by his famous brother. "Powder Your Face with Sunshine" reflected the public personality of the Royal Canadians, Guy Lombardo fans thought his artistry was "The Sweetest Music This Side of Heaven" and a strong incentive to "Get Out Those Old Records" made by the orchestra, and those same fans produced a real "Boo-Hoo" when Guy died. Even when Guy was alive, his music always seemed like old times.

Coquette

A delightful piece with a flirtatious title, "Coquette" (1928), written by musicians Carmen Lombardo and John W. "Johnny" Green (1908-1989) and lyricist Gus Kahn (1886-1941), was a theme of Guy Lombardo and his Royal Canadians. (Whether the group had any claim to royalty is doubtful, but London, Ontario-born Gaetano Alberto Lombardo and his younger brother Carmen were certainly Canadian.) In spite of this close affiliation of band and song, however, Lombardo's orchestra never flirted with audiences, but instead directly and totally immersed them in sweetly performed old-fashioned-style music.

For example, take the songs created by lyricist Kahn with various composers; they definitely tended to be pieces favored by Guy Lombardo fans. With composer Richard A. Whiting and colyricist Raymond B. Egan, Kahn walked the lovely ballad "Some Sunday Morning" (1917) down the aisle. With composer Walter Donaldson, Kahn made several successful musical declarations: "Yes, Sir, That's My Baby" (1925), "My Baby Just Cares for Me" (1930), "My Buddy" (1922, the theme of the Buddy Rogers Orchestra), "Carolina in the Morning" (1922), "Makin' Whoopee" (1928), and "Love Me or Leave Me" (1928). With composer Egbert Van Alstyne, Kahn made us remember the fine nostalgic piece "Memories" (1915), and with Van Alstyne and another composer, Tony Jackson, he noticed a "Pretty Baby" (1916). With composer Ted Fiorito (also known as Ted Fio Rito), Kahn introduced to the world "Charley, My Boy" (1924), and with composer Dan Russo and colyricist Ernie Erdman, he made America familiar with "Toot, Toot, Tootsie" (1922). With composer Nacio Herb Brown, Kahn dreamed up "You Stepped Out of a Dream" (1940). With composer Isham Jones, Kahn had another dream song, "I'll See You in My Dreams" (1924), and another notable love ballad, "It Had to Be You" (1924).

The same situation more or less applies to musician Green. With lyricists Edward Heyman, Robert Sour, and Frank Eyton, he wrote the famous torch song "Body and Soul" (1930), the theme of the Johnny Green Orchestra and the Coleman Hawkins Orchestra; with lyricist Heyman, "Easy Come Easy Go" (1934), "Out of Nowhere" (1931), "You're Mine, You" (1933), and "I Cover the Waterfront" (1933); with lyricists Heyman and Billy Rose, "I Wanna Be Loved" (1933); and with lyricist E. Y. Harburg, "I'm Yours" (1930). The result was several successful songs, mostly compatible with the Royal Canadians, with all earning much green.

Yet from another perspective, all these fine compositions and others, including several more by brother Carmen, have been overshadowed by a much older song closely associated with Guy. "Auld Lang Syne," the anonymous Scottish folk piece from around the seventeenth century whose previously separate words and music were first published together in 1799, was played on radio and television on New Year's Eve for so many years that one could get the impression that the Lombardo Orchestra could not play any other number. "Auld Lang Syne" was much more than a theme of one of the more popular big bands. For Lombardo and many others, it was an entertaining, sweet and tender yearly institution in the same way that Lombardo was a sweet and tender entertainment institution for many, many years.

HAL KEMP
(THE HAL KEMP ORCHESTRA, 1932-1940)

Got a Date with an Angel

Hal Kemp (1905-1940) was far from the best-known leader of a sweet band, although the Hal Kemp Orchestra was a notable ensemble during the 1930s. Even the band's theme "(Oh, How I'll Miss You) When Summer Is Gone" (1937), words and music by Kemp, is far from famous, though adopted by another group, the Tony Barron Orchestra. One of the top hits of the Kemp group, furthermore, was written by artists even less familiar than Kemp. The fine number "Got a Date with an Angel" (1931) was created by obscure lyricists Clifford Grey and Sonnie Miller and obscure musicians Jack Waller and Joseph Tunbridge. ("Date with an Angel" was also the theme of the Skinnay Ennis Orchestra.) Waller and Tunbridge also wrote the music for some lesser-known pieces, including "Hoch Caroline" (1932), words by the also-obscure R. P. Weston (unrelated to bandleader Paul Weston) and Bert Lee; "Sing Brothers" (1932), words by Weston and Lee; and "Roll Away Clouds" (1928) and "My Heart's to Let" (1933), for both of which Waller and Tunbridge also wrote the words.

Two other favorite numbers of the Kemp Orchestra were, in contrast, written by very famous artists. "There's a Small Hotel" (1936) was created by lyricist Lorenz Hart and composer Richard Rodgers. From the 1936 musical *On Your Toes,* "Hotel" was one of the many hits by the top songwriting team of Rodgers and Hart. The other number, "This Year's Kisses," perhaps shared in a small hotel during a date with an angel, was written by the incomparable Irving Berlin for the 1937 musical film *On the Avenue*. That film also included a Berlin classic, "I've Got My Love to Keep Me Warm" (1937), which seems to fit in well with the other three songs.

Hal Kemp was perhaps the least known of the four accomplished sweet band leaders whose last names begin with "K." Sammy Kaye, Kay Kyser, and Wayne King, similar to Kemp, were born in the first decade of the twentieth century but have more enduring reputations, if for no other reason than their lives were more enduring.

HORACE HEIDT (HORACE HEIDT AND HIS CALIFORNIANS AND HORACE HEIDT AND HIS MUSICAL KNIGHTS, 1920s-1945)

Deep in the Heart of Texas

During the late 1930s, Horace Heidt (1901-1986) had a number of hits, including his theme "I'll Love You in My Dreams." This favorable trend continued until the mid-1950s and included a million-disc seller, "Deep in the Heart of Texas." That rousing 1941 novelty that featured hand clapping, written by lyricist June Hersey and musician Don Swander, is still occasionally heard today despite the passing of over a half century. Interestingly, Hersey, who crafted the memorable lines "The moon at night, is big and bright," had not been to Texas prior to 1941.

Another enduring 1940s piece recorded by Heidt was "Don't Fence Me In" (1944), by Cole Porter. (The very talented Porter also wrote "I Love You" [1944], the theme of the Tommy Tucker Orchestra.) Less famous 1940s numbers made into hits by Heidt were the following: "I Don't Want to Set the World on Fire" (1941), by Eddie Seiler, Sol Marcus, Bennie Benjamin, and Eddie Durham, one of Heidt's biggest favorites; "The Shepherd Serenade" (1941), by Kermit Goell and Fred Spielman; "Hut Sut Song" (1941), by

Leo Killian, Ted McMichael, and Jack Owens; and "G'Bye Now" (1941), by Jay Livingston, Ray Evans, Chic Johnson, and Ole Olsen.

The last song was definitely not a classic, but it did have four famous authors. Livingston and Evans were one of the best songwriting teams of the century, and Olsen and Johnson were a very popular and outrageous comedy team in their time and also wrote a few memorable songs. Among their compositions is the goofy and transient "Oh Gee, Oh Gosh, Oh Golly, I'm in Love" (1923), words by Olsen and Johnson, music by Ernest Breuer, which appeared in the *Ziegfeld Follies* of that year. Much better known is the still-performed march "You're in the Army Now" (1929), words by Olsen and Tell Taylor, music by Isham Jones. Taylor also wrote the barbershop classic "Down by the Old Mill Stream" (1910). Jones was also a significant composer and, similar to Horace Heidt, the leader of a top sweet band. For a forgotten song with a short title, "G'Bye Now" certainly has its share of peripheral history.

I'll Love You in My Dreams

Whether they were called Horace Heidt and his Californians or Horace Heidt and his Musical Knights, they were one of the best sweet bands of the 1930s and 1940s. Heidt, born in Alameda, California, also was a significant radio and television star and a frequent utilizer of promotional gimmicks.

Heidt, who led ensembles best described as show bands for listening rather than dance orchestras for dancing, was at his height in the late 1930s. The following were among his 1930s hits: "Gone with the Wind" (1937), words by Herb Magidson, music by Allie Wrubel, a number-one hit which preceded by two years the great movie of the same name and which also was based on the novel by Margaret Mitchell; "Rosalie" (1937), by Cole Porter; "This Can't Be Love" (1938), words by Lorenz Hart, music by Richard Rodgers; "Hot Lips" (1922), by Henry Busse, Henry Lange, and Lou Davis; "Once in a While" (1937), words by Bud Green, music by Michael Edwards; "There's a Gold Mine in the Sky" (1937), by Charles Kenny and Nick Kenny; "Sweet As a Song" (1937), by Mack Gordon and Harry Revel; "Ti-Pi-Tin" (1938), original Spanish lyrics and music by Maria Grever, English lyrics by Raymond Leveen, a top Heidt favorite; "Little Sir Echo" (1917), by Joe Marsala, Laura Smith, J. S. Fearis; "Penny Serenade" (1938), by Arthur William Hallifax and Melle Weersma; and "I'll Love You in My Dreams" (1931), by Abel Baer, Benée Russell, and Horace Heidt.

"I'll Love You" was Heidt's theme song as well as the only notable composition by him. (Baer [1893-1976] did not write a lot, but cowrote the music for "When the One You Love Loves You" [1924] with Paul Whiteman, to accompany the lyrics by Cliff Friend.) As with several other 1930s hits by Heidt, his far-from-famous theme has not endured to the end of the century.

ISHAM JONES
(THE ISHAM JONES ORCHESTRA, EARLY 1920s-1936)

I'll See You in My Dreams

If there was any year that was particularly special for bandleader Isham Jones, it was 1924. He formed a new ensemble that year and also wrote four good songs. "I'll See You in My Dreams" (1924), by lyricist Gus Kahn (1886-1941) and composer Jones (1894-1956), is a fine, ultrasmooth standard and was a top favorite of the Isham Jones Orchestra. The same duo also wrote another preferred piece of the Jones ensemble and an enduring ballad, "It Had to Be You" (1924). (That song, and other contemporary numbers, such as Richard A. Whiting's "Ain't We Got Fun?" [1921], was still being recorded over thirty years later when the Les and Larry Elgart Orchestra recorded it in 1955, along with later pieces, such as "Night Train" [1952], the theme of the Buddy Morrow Orchestra. The music for the 1952 piece was by Jimmy Forrest, the words by Oscar Washington and Lewis C. Simpkins.) At about the same time, Kahn and Jones also created "The One I Love Belongs to Somebody Else" (1924) and "Spain" (1924), one of Jones's themes. Reportedly, the tunes for "It Had to Be," "The One I Love," and "Spain" were created in one all-night session at a piano Jones received from his wife as a thirtieth birthday present. Jones supposedly felt he had to earn more money to pay for the costly gift.

One more notable composition by Kahn and Jones was "Swingin' Down the Lane" (1923), yet another number often performed by the Jones band. "On the Alamo" (1922) was a lesser-known composition by the pair. With other lyricists, Jones wrote "Meet Me in Bubble Land" (1919), words by Caspar Nathan and Joe Manne; "You're Just a Dream Come True" (1931), "If You Were Only Mine" (1932), "I'll Have to Dream Again" (1932), "The Wooden Soldier and the China Doll" (1932), and "You've Got Me Crying Again" (1933), the words for all five by Charles Newman ("You're Just a Dream" was another of Jones's themes); and "You're in the Army Now" (1929), words by Tell Taylor and Ole Olsen.

The last song was somewhat different from Jones's usual love ballads and the softer and sweeter numbers his orchestra tended to perform. A brisk march with comedic lyrics, "You're in the Army Now" shows the influence of Olsen, who was part of the wacky comedy team of Olsen and Johnson. The song also shows the versatility of the musician who, similar to Johnson, had a very common surname, but who also had an uncommon first name and an uncommon talent.

Wabash Blues

"Wabash Blues," a song in honor of a beloved Indiana river, was one of Isham Jones's favorite numbers. He wrote the music for "Indiana Moon" (1923) to go with the lyrics by Benny Davis. One of his most successful recordings, in 1930, was a soft balladlike rendition of "Stardust" (1927), whose very smooth and graceful music was created by Indiana native Hoagy Carmichael. Yet Isham Jones was not born in Indiana nor particularly associated with that Midwestern state so popular with ballad creators, but in Coalton, in adjacent Ohio.

"Wabash Blues" (1921) was written by lyricist Dave Ringle and composer Fred Meinken. Ringle also wrote "Funny Bunny Hug" (1912), with William Tracey and Ray Walker, and added later words to Edward B. Claypoole's 1915 instrumental "Ragging the Scales." "Wabash" was the only top favorite of the Isham Jones Orchestra that was not written by Jones, who was a composer of some accomplishment, especially of songs on the soft, tender, and romantic side.

In 1936, the year that Jones disbanded his band, leading to a new jazz-oriented ensemble led by Woody Herman (a saxophonist with Jones), Isham wrote the music for "There Is No Greater Love," one of his romantic-style compositions. The lyrics were by Marty Symes, and the melody was mostly by Peter Ilich Tchaikovsky (1840-1893), coming from the Russian master's famous Piano Concerto No. 1 (1875). The same work also supplied the music for a better-known derivative, "Tonight We Love" (1941), a popular hit by lyricist Bobby Worth and musicians Ray Austin and Freddy Martin, as well as the theme of the Freddy Martin Orchestra. Whether Jones's atypical decision to borrow a melody from a classical masterpiece rather than create one of his own fine tunes was psychologically related to his decision to dissolve his orchestra at about the same time is something that probably will be never ascertained. However, it is certain that highly talented Jones, who was proficient on several instruments, had one of the best big bands of his time.

JAN GARBER
(THE JAN GARBER ORCHESTRA,
EARLY 1920s-1960s)

A Melody from the Sky

Whether playing jazz-style numbers in the early 1920s using the name Garber Davis Orchestra, or performing swing-style numbers in the early 1940s using the name Jan Garber Orchestra, or playing sweet, syrupy numbers for decades using the once very familiar Jan Garber name, the versatile bands led by Garber earned him the label "the idol of the air lanes." After a few years as a jazz ensemble, the Jan Garber Orchestra followed the lead of the Guy Lombardo Orchestra in the late 1920s and became a sweet band that approached the success of Lombardo's group. Ironically, Garber accomplished this emulation of Canadian Lombardo by becoming the leader of another Canadian sweet band, the Freddie Large Orchestra, of course after changing the group's name.

Garber, however, was not just an imitator of Lombardo, though, similar to the better-known bandleader, he endured in the spotlight for years. With sentimental and soft saxophones, nonbrash brass instruments, and a bit of comedy, Garber made many radio appearances, hence the reputation of air lane idol. The Garber ensemble even was linked with another popular ensemble for a while, George Burns and Gracie Allen, on their radio show during the 1930s.

One of the first numbers headlined by Garber and the Garber Davis group was "When Dixie Stars Are Playing Peek-a-Boo"

(1924), by Al Bernard and J. Russel Robinson. Other 1920s and 1930s numbers performed by Garber included the following: "I Cried for You (Now It's Your Turn to Cry for Me)" (1923), by Arthur Freed, Abe Lyman, and Gus Arnheim (the last two men also becoming bandleaders); the bouncy "I Love My Baby, My Baby Loves Me" (1925), by a pair of noteworthy songwriters, lyricist Bud Green and musician Harry Warren; "Stardust" (1927), the legendary 1927 composition by Hoagy Carmichael, with lyrics added by Mitchell Parish in 1929, which was a favorite of many bands; "Sweet and Hot" (1930), words by Jack Yellen, music by the in-time prominent Harold Arlen; "Sweet and Lovely" (1931), by Arnheim, Harry Tobias, and Jules Lemare; "(On the) Street of Dreams" (1932), by the significant songwriters lyricist Sam M. Lewis and composer Victor Young; the memorable "You Stepped Out of a Dream" (1940), by two more songwriters of importance, lyricist Gus Kahn and composer Nacio Herb Brown; the enduring "Way Down Yonder in New Orleans" (1922), by lyricist Henry Creamer and musician J. Turner Layton; and the perhaps classic "Baby Face" (1926), by lyricist Benny Davis and composer Harry Akst, one of the top numbers of the Garber orchestra. (The 1925 to 1928 period was a fertile time to create musical babies. In addition to the 1926 "Baby Face" and the 1925 "I Love My Baby, My Baby Loves Me" mentioned previously, lyricist Dorothy Fields and musician Jimmy McHugh wrote "I Can't Give You Anything but Love, Baby" in 1928, and Francis Drake "Pat" Ballard wrote "Oh Baby Mine (I Get So Lonely)," also in 1928.)

This sampling of songs recorded by Garber suggests that his ensembles put many melodies in the sky. Garber also took a melody from the sky, that is, adopted a piece of that name as possibly his favorite number. "A Melody from the Sky," a typical sweet band composition, was written in 1936 by lyricist Sidney D. Mitchell and composer Louis Alter. That not very famous duo also wrote "You Turned the Tables on Me" (1936) and "Twilight on the Trail" (1936), which suggests it is time to end for now.

You're Breaking My Heart

The Jan Garber Orchestra was one of the longest-lasting of the big bands, as well as one of the best sweet bands. Garber (1897-1977), a violinist born in Morristown, Pennsylvania, led the ensemble for many years, on two occasions (the early 1920s and 1942-1945) leading it as a predominantly jazz band. His name has continued on in the form of a 1990s Milwaukee-based group still bearing the Garber name and still performing a wide variety of numbers in the spirit of Garber's appealing mix of love songs, waltzes, dance songs, college songs, and jazz.

Perhaps the most notable year for Garber was 1949. The Garber orchestra had two hit records that year, "You're Breaking My Heart" and "Jealous Heart," and appeared in the film *Make Believe Ballroom* along with the Jimmy Dorsey Orchestra and the Charlie Barnet Orchestra. The dramatic "Breaking" was written in 1948 by Pat Genaro and Sunny Skylar, based on the song "La Mattinata" from the 1904 opera *Der Roland von Berlin* by Italian composer Ruggero Leoncavallo (1858-1919), who is best known for his dramatic 1892 opera *Pagliacci* and its crying, broken-hearted clown scene. Leoncavallo's song is also known under the title "Tis the Day." Genaro also wrote another "heart" song, "Here in My Heart" (1952), with Lou Levinson and Bill Borelli. The other heart song mentioned previously, "Jealous Heart" (1944), by Jenny Lou Carson, was most popular in 1949 when recorded by Garber. Carson's best-known song, probably, is her passionate "Let Me Go Lover" (1955), words by Al Hill, music by Carson. (Originally, Carson's "lover" was a "devil," for the first [1953] version of the lyrics by Carson was "Let Me Go Devil.")

When not playing "heart" songs, the fine Garber ensemble recorded numbers such as his theme song "My Dear," by Garber and Freddie Large, recorded around 1948; the tender "Shadow of Your Smile" (1965), the Oscar and Grammy winner by lyricist Paul Francis Webster and composer Johnny Mandel; the boisterous jazz favorite "Stomping at the Savoy" (1936), words by Andy Razaf, music by Benny Goodman, Edgar Sampson, and Chick Webb; and the more restrained jazz number "The Soft Shoe Shuffle" (1942), by Spencer Williams and Maurice Berman.

KAY KYSER
(THE KAY KYSER ORCHESTRA, EARLY 1930s-EARLY 1950s)

Three Little Fishes

Laughs, little things, and alliteration seem to have been a focus of the Kay Kyser Orchestra. "Three Little Fishes," "Woody Woodpecker," and "Jingle, Jangle, Jingle" were favorite numbers of James Kern Kyser (1906-1985), who changed his artistic name to Kay Kyser, quite possibly to take advantage of the catchy sound of matching first letters.

"Three Little Fishes" (1939), by Saxie Dowell, musically portrayed the tale of three baby fishes and a mother fish that swam right over a dam. "Woody Woodpecker" (1947), based on Walter Lantz's famous cartoon character, was written by George Tibbles and Ramey Idriss. (Some persons say that Kyser actually wrote the 1947 novelty. If he did, he used a pseudonym, either Tibbles or Idriss or both.) That novelty mimicked the shrill, rapid-fire, taunting laugh that was the core of the personality of the hyperactive woodpecker, a sound created and performed by Lantz's wife in the popular animated cartoons. "Jingle, Jangle, Jingle" (1942, words by Frank Loesser, music by Joseph J. Lilley), which amusingly told of spurs that jingle, jangle, jingle, was yet another novelty performed by the frequently lighthearted Kyser ensemble.

Kyser also performed more serious songs, including one of the band's top numbers, "Praise the Lord and Pass the Ammunition"

(1942), a World War II era hit. The creator of this notable patriotic song was the very notable songwriter Frank Loesser. Yet even "Praise the Lord" had a widely used and appealing performance gimmick, involving male choral voices that rhythmically produced a striking musical aura of power and determination.

In summary, the Kay Kyser Orchestra was a lovable group with a good sense of humor as well as the talent to offer one of the best sweet bands of the midcentury period. As one of their hit recordings, a 1942 composition by Bill Carey and Carl Fischer, proclaimed, "Who Wouldn't Love You?" In part this gushing sentiment reflected the kind thoughts of Kyser's theme song, "Thinking of You," written in 1927 by lyricist Bert Kalmar and composer Harry Ruby.

LAWRENCE WELK
(THE LAWRENCE WELK
ORCHESTRA, 1925-1970s,
1955-1982 ON TELEVISION)

Don't Sweetheart Me

Lawrence Welk (1903-1992) was an American national phenomenon. He was widely criticized for playing supposedly corny and watered-down music, which he called champagne music. (Welk actually wrote the music for a work with "champagne" in its title, "Champagne Polka" [1945], words by Norman Lee, which he often performed.) He was somewhat ill at ease on camera and never fully mastered English pronunciation (despite being born in Strasburg, North Dakota). Yet *The Lawrence Welk Show* was on television regularly for twenty-seven years (1955-1982, the last eleven years in syndication) and was more than occasionally seen in reruns throughout the 1990s.

An accordion player, Welk formed a dance band around 1925, becoming the leader of a very popular radio orchestra in the 1930s. Throughout his over fifty years in the business, he retained his policy of presenting music that reflected his German ancestry, that is, waltzes, love ballads, popular excerpts from classical compositions, and similar mainstream or conservative numbers. For instance, when Welk recorded a song with "gypsy" in the title, it was not a wild, esoteric dance but instead the relatively bland Bing Crosby favorite

"Gypsy in My Soul" (1937), words by Moe Jaffe and Clay Boland, music by Boland. When he went outside of these parameters, for example, into jazz, the melodies were transformed into his bland, yet successful style that was simple, direct, and unassuming. (Incidentally, "welk" is a German word meaning "limp," "flabby," and "languid.")

During the period from 1956 to 1972, more or less the time he was on network television, forty-two of his albums made the weekly lists of top hits. His biggest hit, ironically, was a rock song, though a soft one. "Calcutta" (1960), words by Lee Pockriss and Paul J. Vance, music by Heino Gaze, was number one in Welk's rendition for eleven weeks during 1961. Of the immense number of other songs performed by the Lawrence Welk Orchestra on radio, television, or record, two pieces particularly stand out: "Bubbles in the Wine" (1939), by the later Broadway music master Frank Loesser (1910-1969), Bob Calamé, and Welk, was the very familiar theme heard for years on television, and another top favorite, the somewhat later composition "Don't Sweetheart Me" (1943), by Cliff Friend (1893-1974) and Charles Tobias (1898-1970), both songwriters of some importance. The previous three songs typify his wide repertory. "Calcutta" was an example of how he used songs normally outside of his range of interest to his advantage, "Bubbles in the Wine" was the symbol of his frothy "champagne music," and "Don't Sweetheart Me" was a prime example of the romantic compositions that were Welk's ongoing staple.

LEO REISMAN
(THE LEO REISMAN ORCHESTRA,
MID-1920s–EARLY 1940s)

The Continental

The classic dance piece "The Continental" was a very suitable number for the sophisticated and continental audiences for which the Leo Reisman Orchestra generally played. Written by lyricist Herb Magidson (1906-) and composer Con Conrad (1891-1938), and introduced in the 1934 film *The Gay Divorcée,* "Continental" won the first Academy Award for best film song. Conrad also wrote both words and music for "You Call It Madness (Ah, But I Call It Love)" (1931), the theme of both the Don Glasser Orchestra and the Russ Carlyle Orchestra. Two other themes of Carlyle were "If I Ever Love Again" (1949), by Carlyle and Dick Reynolds, and "In the Chapel in the Moonlight" (1936), by Billy Hill.

Also in the same film as "The Continental" was another classic, "Night and Day," which first appeared in the 1932 Broadway musical *Gay Divorce.* "Night and Day" was another favorite of the Reisman Orchestra, which made hit recordings of that piece and "I've Got You on My Mind," which was from the same 1932 musical. (Debonaire Fred Astaire was the vocalist with the Reisman ensemble for both numbers.) The lyricist and composer for "Night and Day" and "I've Got You on My Mind" was the great creator of sophisticated musicals, Cole Porter. Porter also wrote another "I've Got You" composition, the standard "I've Got You Under My Skin"

(1936), and Reisman's theme, "What Is This Thing Called Love?" (1930).

Reisman (1897-1961) also recorded the classics "Dancing in the Dark" (1931), by lyricist Howard Dietz and composer Arthur Schwartz, and "Stormy Weather" (1933), by lyricist Ted Koehler and composer Harold Arlen. Whereas "Dancing" is a smooth, moody, and erotic dance number, "Stormy" can perhaps best be described as a sensitive, sophisticated, and high-class blues number. Among the persons who have recorded "Stormy" are Arlen, himself, who performed vocals with the Reisman ensemble and the celebrated African-American vocalists Lena Horne and Ethel Waters. The latter singer introduced "Stormy" at well-known jazz mecca the Cotton Club in Harlem. Although race relations during the 1930s, as in other times, were often stormy, cultural streams sometimes allowed for the free flow of good music between the white and black communities.

Paradise

Leo Reisman did not have a typical background for a popular bandleader. A violinist born in Boston, he attended the New England Conservatoire of Music and joined the Baltimore Symphony Orchestra at age eighteen. Around 1919, he formed a dance orchestra that performed at Boston's Hotel Brunswick. In time, the Leo Reisman Orchestra became a resident at the very high-class Waldorf Astoria Hotel in New York City, as well as a respected, nationally known society dance band, partly via the medium of radio.

Although the Reisman group did record some jazz-oriented numbers, they preferred the standard popular repertory, including film and Broadway musical compositions. Three of Reisman's favorite numbers, probably not by accident, were by the same composer, Nacio Herb Brown (1896-1964). "Paradise," or "Paradise Waltz," was written by Brown in 1931, with Gordon Clifford producing the lyrics. "The Wedding of the Painted Doll" (1929) was written by Brown with lyricist Arthur Freed for the 1929 film *Broadway Melody*. That movie also included another Reisman favorite, "You Were Meant for Me," the title song "Broadway Melody," both by Brown and Freed, and George M. Cohan's classic 1904 number "Give My Regards to Broadway."

"Paradise," "Painted Doll," and "Broadway Melody" have not well-survived the test of time. Far more enduring are the standard "You Were Meant for Me" and the classic "Singin' in the Rain," which was written by Brown and Freed for another 1929 film, *Hollywood Revue of 1929*. Another film with "Hollywood" in the title was *Going Hollywood* (1933), in which Bing Crosby introduced the excellent perennial "Temptation," also by Brown and Freed. This duo also wrote other noteworthy songs, including the theme of the Enoch Light Orchestra, "My Lucky Star," or "You Are My Lucky Star" (1935). We will, however, avoid the temptation to mention them all here.

PAUL WHITEMAN
(THE PAUL WHITEMAN ORCHESTRA, 1918-1938, OCCASIONALLY REGROUPED UNTIL 1942)

Whispering

If there ever was any doubt that the Paul Whiteman Orchestra was more of a sweet band than a jazz ensemble, in spite of Whiteman's extensive promotion of jazz, the adoption of "Whispering" as a favorite Whiteman number should have settled that debate. Tenuously tender and slowly sliding, "Whispering" (1920, words by Malvin Schonberger, music by John Schonberger) is perhaps too far removed from the styles of jazz to be successfully converted to it. Also in the same general mode was another Whiteman favorite, "Linger Awhile" (1923), a love ballad by lyricist Harry Owens and composer Vincent Rose. Owens and Rose were also bandleaders, with the Harry Owens Orchestra adopting Owen's 1937 composition "Sweet Leilani" as its theme and the Vincent Rose Orchestra preferring "Linger Awhile."

Other songs performed by Whiteman (1890-1967) included the following: "Song of the Dawn" (1930), words by Jack Yellen, music by Milton Ager; "I'll Never Be the Same" (1932), words by Gus Kahn, music by Matt Malneck and Frank Signorelli; "Stairway to the Stars" (1935), words by Mitchell Parish, music by Malneck and Signorelli; "My Blue Heaven" (1927), words by Richard A. Whiting, music by Walter Donaldson; "At Sundown" (1927), by Donaldson; "Ramona" (1927), words by L. Wolfe Gilbert, music by Mabel Wayne; "Just an Echo in the Valley" (1932), by James Campbell, Reginald Connelly, and Harry Woods; "In a Little Spanish Town" (1926), words by Sam M. Lewis and Joe Young, music by Wayne; "I'm Through with Love" (1931), words by Kahn, music by Malneck and Fud Livingston; "Do You Ever Think of Me?" (1920), by Harry D. Kerr and Earl Burnett; and "Rose Room" (1917), by Harry Williams and Art Hickman, the theme of the Art Hickman Orchestra and the closing theme of the Phil Harris Orchestra. Another "rose" song, "Honeysuckle Rose" (1929), words by Andy Razaf, music by Thomas "Fats" Waller, was a theme of the Coleman Hawkins Orchestra.

Perhaps as an indirect tribute to the African-American origins of jazz, Whiteman, in 1932, recorded several pre-jazz era black spirituals. These included "Goin' to the Promised Lan'," "On Revival Day," "Ain't Done Nothin' But Pray," "Moan, You Moaners!," "When Gabriel Blows That Horn," "Pray, Children, Pray," "Glory!," "Is There a Place Up There for Me?," "Children, Walk with Me," and "There's Religion in Rhythm." The last song could have been a credo of Paul Whiteman, who almost made a religion out of his strong support for jazz.

Wonderful One

The Paul Whiteman Orchestra was a combination jazz and sweet band, with overall stronger leanings toward sweet. The theme of the Whiteman ensemble, "Rhapsody in Blue" (1924) also had a dual personality of jazz and classical modes, with the jazz aspects dominating overall. Whiteman led the orchestra in New York City on the landmark day that the great George Gershwin (1898-1937) first publicly played the piano sections of his "Rhapsody." One of the most important compositions of the century, "Rhapsody" has been widely recorded, including by the Freddy Martin Orchestra, which rendered it in a style more sweet than jazzy.

Whiteman, born in Denver, Colorado, was one of the most influential musicians of his era and helped introduce jazz to the general public, although in a somewhat watered-down or sanitized form. He was given the label "The king of jazz," a somewhat misleading or exaggerated claim. Although he strongly supported the new jazz idiom, his favorite numbers often reflected his tendencies toward softer numbers. Among the Whiteman favorites was "(My) Wonderful One" (1922), a waltz created by lyricist Dorothy Terriss and musicians Whiteman and Ferde Grofé (1892-1972). Grofé made the first orchestration of "Rhapsody," with Gershwin himself making a later one. Gershwin, Whiteman, and Grofé also merged their talents in 1926 when the Whiteman Orchestra performed Gershwin's instrumental "Blue Monday" (1922) in New York's Carnegie Hall using a new arrangement by Grofé. "My Wonderful One" could have partially been a tribute by Whiteman to the genius of Gershwin, or it could be a description of Gershwin's feelings toward his mentor Whiteman.

Dorothy Terriss (1890-1953), also known as Dorothy Terris, Theodora Morse, and Dolly Morse, helped to write another top Whiteman favorite in waltz style, "Three O'Clock in the Morning" (1921), words by Terriss, music by Julian Robledo. Terriss, in addition, created the English lyrics for "Siboney" (1929), original Spanish lyrics and music by Ernesto Lecuona. Other songs performed by Whiteman during the 1920s included "I Never Knew I Could Love Anybody Like I'm Loving You," or "I Never Knew" (1920), by Tom Pitts, Raymond B. Egan, and Roy K. Marsh (revised by Whiteman); and "Play That Song of India Again" (1921), words by Leo Wood and Irving Bibo, music adapted by Whiteman from Nikolay Rimsky-Korsakov's 1888 classical work *Sheherazade*. The same music was utilized over a decade later, in 1937, when the Tommy Dorsey Orchestra, in its heyday as outstanding a swing band as Whiteman's group were a sweet band, recorded the instrumental hit "Song of India."

SAMMY KAYE
(THE SAMMY KAYE ORCHESTRA, 1935-1975)

Daddy

Although the promotions for the Sammy Kaye Orchestra proclaimed "swing and sway with Sammy Kaye," there was little or no swing in the sense of big band jazz. One could sway to his simple and sweet sounds, but hot or even fairly warm jazz was, as a whole, foreign to the Kaye repertory. He did occasionally play his version of Dixieland numbers, however.

Despite criticism that his band was "corny" and "unoriginal," Kaye's ensemble survived for decades. Kaye (1910-   ), born in Lakewood, Ohio, was a very able clarinettist, hired good musicians, and knew how to effectively use gimmicks such as, "So you want to lead a band." Employed on both his radio and later television programs, Kaye's invitation to be a bandleader actually allowed persons in the audience to conduct the orchestra for a while. Kaye also was a modestly successful songwriter. He and Don Reid wrote "Remember Pearl Harbor" (1941), an important patriotic song of the World War II period, and "Until Tomorrow" (1940), one of his themes. Kaye also wrote "Kaye's Melody," probably during the early 1940s, which became his number-one theme. In addition, Sammy and Billy Kaye collaborated on the lyrics of "Hawaiian Sunset" (1940), with Sammy providing the music. Don Reid,

Kaye's top collaborator, also wrote "Green Years" (1954), with Arthur Altman.

Other than the songs by Kaye, one of top favorites of the Kaye ensemble was a composition by two obscure songwriters. "Daddy" (1941), which should not be confused with the better-known composition "My Heart Belongs to Daddy" (1938), by Cole Porter, was created by Lou Klein and Robert Trout for the 1941 film *Two Latins from Manhattan*. Klein also wrote "A Gay Caballero" (1928), with Frank Crumit; "If I Had My Way" (1913), words by Klein, music by James Kendis; and the forgettable but interestingly titled "She Lived Next Door to a Firehouse" (1931), with Fred Phillips. The most notable song connected with any of these men is perhaps "I'm Forever Blowing Bubbles" (1918), for which Kendis collaborated on the words with the also obscure James Brockman and Nat Vincent, with the melody created by the equally obscure John William Kellette. Although some of Kaye's numbers, including "Daddy," have been more or less forgotten, even by the daddies and mommies who lived during the 1940s, the name of Sammy Kaye lives on, at least for a while.

Harbor Lights

The term "harbor" is not often found in song titles, yet, curiously, it appears in two of the favorite pieces of bandleader Sammy Kaye. "Remember Pearl Harbor" (1941), by Kaye and Don Reid, is perhaps Kaye's best-known composition. "Harbor Lights" (1937), words by Jimmy Kennedy (1903?-1984), music by Will Grosz (1894-1939) (also known as Hugh Williams), was one of the favorite numbers of the Sammy Kaye Orchestra. (You can bet that Pearl Harbor in Hawaii did not have any lights at night for quite a while after its bombing by the Japanese on December 7, 1941.)

"Harbor Lights" was successfully revived in 1950 and 1960. Also revived in 1960 was another song with "light" in its title that was also a Kaye favorite, "The Old Lamp Lighter." That composition was written in 1946 by lyricist Charles Tobias and composer Nat Simon. Tobias and Simon coproduced several other songs, including "The Mama Doll Song" (1954), "No Can Do" (1945), and "Coax Me a Little Bit" (1946). Simon also had other collaborators, including Buddy Bernier, who helped create "Poinciana" (1936), plus the aforementioned Jimmy Kennedy. Demonstrating the complex and sometimes circular relationships of songwriters, one favorite of Kaye was cowritten by Kennedy and another by Simon, and the two artists also cowrote with each other. Lyricist Kennedy and musician Simon as a team produced "And Mimi" (1947), "Sweet Heartaches" (1956), and the hysterical historical novelty "Istanbul (Not Constantinople)" (1954), which related the reason "you can't go back to Constantinople" (the city's name was changed).

But Kaye's group and other bands did go back in time on occasion. In the middle of the century, Kaye recorded a composition from the beginning of the century, "Melody of Love." One of several songs with that title or with that phrase in the lyrics, this specific number was written in 1903 by lyricist Tom Glazer and musician Hans Engelmann. The Wayne King Orchestra, more or less a contemporary ensemble with Kaye's, also recorded "Melody of Love," thus helping to demonstrate that there is plenty of melody and plenty of love to go around.

SHEP FIELDS
(SHEP FIELDS AND HIS RIPPLING RHYTHM, 1934-1939)

Did I Remember?

It is not easy to remember the several names given to ensembles led by Shep Fields. Born in Brooklyn, New York, Fields (1910-), a saxophone and clarinet player, led Shep Fields and his Rippling Rhythm in the 1930s, which often appeared on the radio; Shep Fields and his New Music in the early 1940s; and the Shep Fields Orchestra in the late 1940s and early 1950s. (The rippling rhythm technique supposedly was a simulation of the sound made by blowing through a straw immersed in a container of water.)

Perhaps to help one's memory, Fields had several hits that suggest the process of mental recall. "Did I Remember?" (1936), perhaps Fields's top hit, was written by lyricist Harold Adamson (1906-) and composer Walter Donaldson (1893-1947). (Adamson, Edwin Knopf, and Jack King also collaborated on the theme of the Art Jarrett Orchestra, "Ev'rything's Been Done Before" [1935].) Another top hit, and also the theme of comedian Bob Hope, was "Thanks for the Memory" (1937), by lyricist Leo Robin and composer Ralph Rainger. (Robin and Rainger also created the theme of the Muzzy Marcelino Orchestra, "I'll Take an Option on You" [1933].) Other Fields hits hinting of memory were "This Year's Kisses" (1937) by Irving Berlin; "The Merry Go Round Broke Down" (1937), by Cliff Friend and Dave Franklin; "That Old Feeling" (1937), by lyricist Lew Brown and composer Sammy Fain; and "South of the Border, Down Mexico Way" (1939), by Jimmy Kennedy and Michael Carr, a top Fields favorite that told of a past romance. ("The Merry Go Round Broke Down" is also tied to fond memories of old Warner Brothers cartoons that used it as their closing theme.)

Additional hits by Fields not particularly associated with memory were "Whistle While You Work" (1937), by lyricist Larry Morey and composer Frank Churchill, from the Disney animated classic *Snow White and the Seven Dwarfs;* "Moonlight and Shadows" (1936), by Robin and Frederick Hollander, from the film *Jungle Princess;* "There's Something in the Air" (1937), words by Adamson, music by Jimmy McHugh, from the film *Banjo on My Knee;* and "Cathedral in the Pines" (1938), by Charles Kenny and Nick Kenny. Although Fields is not personally well remembered in the late twentieth century, some of his favorite numbers include "South of the Border," "That Old Feeling," "Whistle While You Work," "Moonlight and Shadows," and "Thanks for the Memory." Thanks for the memories, Shep.

WAYNE KING
(THE WAYNE KING ORCHESTRA,
EARLY 1920s-1945,
SEMIACTIVE THROUGH THE 1960s)

Beautiful Love

The Wayne King Orchestra played beautiful music for many years. Among the numerous numbers wafting from the King ensemble was "Beautiful Love" (1931), music by King (1901-1985), Victor Young (1900-1956), and Egbert Van Alstyne (1882-1951), words by Haven Gillespie (1888-1975). (Another song by Gillespie, "Breezin' Along with the Breeze" [1926], with Seymour Simons and Richard A. Whiting, was the theme of the Lou Breese Orchestra.) "Beautiful" was perhaps the second favorite number of King after his theme "The Waltz You Saved for Me" (1930), words by Gus Kahn, music by King and Emil Flindt. (Another sweet band led by a musician named King, incidentally, was the Henry King Orchestra, whose theme was "A Blues Serenade," written in 1935 by lyricist Mitchell Parish and composer Frank Signorelli. Henry King [1906-1974], a pianist, led a society ensemble. Yet another King associated with a big band theme was Charles E. King, who wrote "Song of the Islands" [1915], the theme of the Ben Pollack Orchestra. While we are on the subject of kings, the theme of the Al King Orchestra was "It's No Fun" or "It's No Fun Dancing If the Band Don't Swing" [1936], by Milton Ager, Murray Mencher, and Charles Newman.)

Wayne King also recorded several other songs with "beautiful" or "love" in the titles, including the following: "I'd Love to Live in Loveland (with a Girl Like You)" (1910), by W. R. Williams; "Melody of Love" (1903), words by Tom Glazer, music by Hans Engelmann; "The Night Is Young and You're So Beautiful" (1936), words by Irving Kahal and Billy Rose, music by Dana Suesse; "We Could Make Such Beautiful Music (Together)" (1940), words by Robert Sour, music by Henry Manners; and "Je Vous Aime" (in English, "I Love You"), written in 1947 by Sam Coslow.

Wayne King also recorded numbers that only implied beauty and/or romance, such as the following: "Castle of Dreams" (1919), words by Joseph McCarthy, music by Harry Tierney; "Remember" (1925), by Irving Berlin; "Time Was," or "Dreaming" (1941), original Spanish lyrics ("Duerme") by Gabriel Luna, English lyrics by Sidney Keith Russell, music by Miguel Prado; "My Man" (1921), original French lyrics by Albert Willemetz, English lyrics by Channing Pollock, music by Maurice Yvain; "Trust in Me" (1936), by Ned Wever and Jean Schwartz; "Wabash Moon" (1931), by Dave Dreyer and Morton Downey (Dreyer also wrote the music for "Cecilia" [1925], words by Herman Ruby, the theme of the Ronnie Kemper Orchestra); "You Walk by" (1940), by Ben Raleigh and Bernie Wayne; and "To You Sweetheart, Aloha" (1936), by Harry Owens.

If the last song is somewhat reminiscent of another song saying goodbye to one's sweetheart, there is good reason. One of Wayne King's top favorites was "Goodnight, Sweetheart" (1931), by Ray Noble, James Campbell, and Reginald Connelly, the closing theme of the Ray Noble Orchestra.

The Waltz You Saved for Me

The original "waltz king" was the Viennese master Johann Strauss Jr. (1825-1899). Another notable "waltz king" was American bandleader and saxophonist Wayne King. If one believes in reincarnation, there is the possibility that the twentieth-century King is a later human manifestation of the nineteenth-century "king." After all, the latter musician was born a short time after Strauss died and his initials were "W. K.," which could also be an omen of the arrival of a new "waltz king."

Whether the previous speculation has any validity or not, Wayne King was the leader of a very successful sweet band. Appropriately, the theme of the Wayne King Orchestra was "The Waltz You Saved for Me" (1930). Written by King with cocomposer Emil Flindt and lyricist Gus Kahn (1886-1941), this lovely "waltz ballad" was just one of several compositions by King. Among the other better-known pieces by King were "Beautiful Love" (1931), words by Haven Gillespie, music by Victor Young, Egbert Van Alstyne, and King; "Goofus" (1930), words by Kahn, music by King and William Harold; and "Josephine" (1937), words by Kahn, music by King and Burke Bivens.

Lesser-known compositions by King include the following: "Blue Hours" (1933), words by Roy Turk, music by King and Jerry Castillo; "Corn Walk" (1940), words by Irving Kahal, music by King and Hall Bellis; "Hula Lou" (1924), by Jack Yellen, Milton Charles, and King; "So Close to Me" (1931), by King, Castillo, and Chester Cohn; and "That Little Boy of Mine" (1929), by Benny Meroff, Walter Hirsch, and King. Since King was not a highly productive composer, wrote no real classics, and, for all the songs mentioned thus far, worked with collaborators, he could not be fairly described as the twentieth-century king of waltz composition. (That title might be claimed by Richard Rodgers or Irving Berlin.) But he definitely was one of the twentieth-century kings of waltz performance. The following were among the many waltzes recorded by the King orchestra: "Alice Blue Gown," or "In My Sweet Alice Blue Gown" (1919), words by Joseph McCarthy, music by Harry Tierney (the same duo wrote "Rio Rita" [1926], the theme of the Ted Fio Rito Orchestra); "Let's Dance" (1935), words by Joseph Bonine and Gregory Stone, music by Fanny Baldridge (the theme of the Benny Goodman Orchestra); "Anniversary Waltz" (1941), by Dave Franklin and Al Dubin; "What'll I Do?" (1924), by Irving Berlin; and, in honor of his waltz predecessor, "Blue Danube" (1867), by Johann Strauss Jr.

XAVIER CUGAT
(XAVIER CUGAT'S ORCHESTRA—
UNDER SEVERAL NAMES, INCLUDING
THE WALDORF ASTORIA ORCHESTRA,
EARLY 1920s-LATE 1950s
OR EARLY 1960s)

Brazil

When your name is Francisco de Asis Javier Cugat Mingall de Bru y Deluefeo, it is no wonder why it was shortened to Xavier Cugat. Born in Gerona, Spain, Cugat (1900-1990) became skilled on the violin in Cuba where he was raised and played in concert halls and clubs. After emigrating to the United States in 1921, he formed a musical ensemble, Xavier Cugat and his Gigolos, which appeared in several early 1930s films. In the mid-1930s, Cugat switched to being the leader of the Waldorf Astoria Orchestra in New York City. Not long after, Cugat adopted the lively "The Lady in Red" as one of his very top numbers. Written in 1935 by Mort Dixon and Allie Wrubel, "Lady" was somewhat atypical for Cugat; that is, it was not of Latin American origins.

Because of his cultural background, Cugat tended to specialize in tangos and other Latin American modes, all to great audience approval. During the 1940s and 1950s, he was fairly often seen in films and even on television. Among his hits in the 1940s were "Brazil," which honored that large and musically productive nation, and "Walter Winchell Rhumba," which honored a famous newscaster of the period. "Brazil," a top favorite of Cugat, was written by musician Ary Barroso in 1939, with English lyrics derived from the original Portuguese lyrics, "Arquelo do Brasil," by Sidney Keith "Bob" Russell. It was a big hit in 1943. Another song by Barroso (1903-1964), again with a Brazilian theme, was "Baia" (1944), music by Barroso, English lyrics by Ray Gilbert. "Walter Winchell Rhumba" (1946) was by lyricist Carl Sigman and composer Noro Morales.

Cugat also did some composing. In 1934, he wrote the music for his theme, "My Shawl," original Spanish lyrics by Pedro Berrios, English lyrics by Stanley Adams. In 1942, three years before "My Shawl" was successfully revived in 1945, Cugat, George Roser, and Fred Wise created "Nightingale," which had no obvious connections to Latin America or Spain. Cugat's music, however, though not entirely authentic Latin American, was for about two generations closely connected to the fountain of melody and rhythm emanating from south of the Rio Grande.

The Breeze and I

One of the top hits by the very popular Xavier Cugat was "The Breeze and I." Sung by Dinah Shore in 1940, "Breeze" was written that year by lyricist Al Stillman (1906-1979) and musician Ernesto Lecuona (1896-1963). The melody was derived from Lecuona's 1930 suite *Andalucia,* which also was the source of another popular song by Lecuona, "Andalucia."

The best-known song by Lecuona is perhaps the dramatic "Malagueña" (1930), Spanish lyrics and music by Lecuona, later English lyrics by Marian Banks. Other notable Lecuona compositions include the following: "Siboney" (1929), Spanish lyrics and music by Lecuona, English lyrics by Dorothy Terriss; "Say Si Si" (1936), Spanish lyrics by Francia Lubin, English lyrics by Stillman, music by Lecuona; "(You Are) Always in My Heart" (1942), words by Kim Gannon, music by Lecuona; "African Lament" ("Lamento Africano") (1931), words by L. Wolfe Gilbert, music by Lecuona; "Two Hearts That Pass in the Night" (1941), words by Forman Brown, music by Lecuona; and "Jungle Drums" ("Canto Karabali") (1933), English lyrics by Carmen Lombardo and Charles O'Flynn, music by Lecuona.

Lecuona and Cugat had a lot in common besides Cugat's successful use of Lecuona's "The Breeze and I." Lecuona was born in Guanabacoa, Cuba; Cugat grew up in that nation. They both were born about the same time (Cugat in 1900), they both moved to the United States and worked for a while in New York City, and they both became composers and bandleaders. Cugat's ensembles were more famous than Lecuona and his Cuban Boys, another Latin American dance band, but Lecuona was by far the more accomplished composer. As suggested by the "cu" in both their names, they both had a lot of Cuba in their artistic veins.

SOME UNHERALDED BANDS

BENNIE MOTEN
(BENNIE MOTEN'S KANSAS CITY
ORCHESTRA, CIRCA 1922-1935)

Moten Swing

One of the earliest uses of the term "swing" in the title of a song, when relating to jazz, was in the lively number "Moten Swing," which was written in 1933. (Another early similar use of "swing" was in the 1932 stick of dynamite "It Don't Mean a Thing If It Ain't Got That Swing," words by Irving Mills, music by Duke Ellington.) Also known as "Moten's Swing," the 1933 piece was created by Bennie Moten (1894-1935) and his brother Buster Moten. In that same year, accordionist Buster and saxophonist Eddie Barefield wrote another jazz composition, "Toby."

"Moten Swing" was one of the themes of Bennie Moten's Kansas City Orchestra, one of the first outstanding and famous African-American ensembles. Born in Kansas City, Missouri, Moten was a pianist of some reputation when he formed his band in 1920, or somewhat before. The Moten group helped to establish Kansas City as a top center for first-rate jazz. Moten attracted some excellent players, including William Basie, who later took over the band after Moten's untimely death due to a surgical error. "Count" Basie continued Moten's pioneering work of combining the musical ideas of New Orleans with the modes of the Midwest and probably brought Kansas City jazz to its zenith.

Another favorite number of the Moten band was the charming and sort of circular-rhythmed "South" (1924), an instrumental by Moten and Thamon Hayes. "South" was recorded in 1924 and again in 1928. (Ray Charles added lyrics later.) The Moten ensemble also recorded a number of other jazz compositions in the late 1920s than are less known than "South": "Moten Stomp" (1927), by Moten and Hayes, an earlier version of "Moton Swing," and an earlier theme, with which was issued "Blue Guitar Stomp" (1927), by Cal Smith, performed by Clifford Hayes' Louisville Stompers; yet another stomp, "Terrific Stomp" (1929), by Moten and Booker Washington, which was issued again seven years later in 1936, accompanied by "It's Tight Like That," by Dorsey Whittaker, a favorite number of another African-American band, McKinney's Cotton Pickers (their theme song was "If I Could Be with You One Hour Tonight" [1926], by Henry Creamer and Jimmy P. Johnson); yet another song with "Moten" in the title, "Moten's Blues," or "Moten Blues" (1929), by Moten alone; "Kansas City Shuffle" (1927), by Moten alone; and "Kansas City Squabble" (1929), by Moten and Ed Lewis. In all, Moten brought a lot of life to Kansas City decades before Detroit became the musical "Motown" in the 1960s.

BENNY CARTER
(THE BENNY CARTER ORCHESTRA, 1933-1934, 1938-1940, 1943-1945)

Kansas City Suite

Kansas City, Missouri, has several significant associations with music. In the 1920s and 1930s, it was a major mecca for jazz musicians, including prominent artists such as Bennie Moten and Count Basie. It also has been honored by two notable songs, one in mainstream pops style and the other in classic rock style. "Kansas City" was a lively extended dance number in the Broadway musical *Oklahoma!* (1943), by composer Richard Rodgers and lyricist Oscar Hammerstein II. It described, tongue in cheek, about how everything was "up to date in Kansas City." A later "Kansas City" was a top rock song in 1959, written by the very successful songwriting team of lyricist Mike Stoller and musician Jerry Leiber. It described how the singer was "goin' to Kansas City," perhaps reminiscent of many jazz musicians of about a generation earlier.

Less famous, but still of some consequence, is *Kansas City Suite* by Benny Carter, a jazz suite recorded in 1958 by the Count Basie Orchestra. (Carter had done some composing before this, including "Melancholy Lullaby," written with Edward Heyman no later than 1939, and "Malibu" [recorded 1945], by Carter alone. These two numbers were themes of the Benny Carter Orchestra, and "Melancholy" was also recorded by the Hal Kemp and Glenn Miller Orchestras.) Drawing on his own experiences with the jazz center,

Carter wrote ten sections: "Vine Street Rumble," "Katy-Do," "Miss Missouri," "Jackson County Jubilee," "Sunset Glow," "The Wiggle Walk," "Meetin' Time," "Paseo Promenade," "Blue Five Jive," and "Rompin' at the Reno." In these numbers, which were performed by the Carter ensemble as well as the Basie group, Carter captured several images that can be associated with jazz: rumble, jubilee, glow, wiggle, walk, meetin', promenade, blue, jive, and rompin'. Kansas City must have been quite a place between World War I and World War II, a creative oasis of compelling sound wedged in between the nonproductive deserts of the two conflicts.

When the Lights Are Low

Leaders of big bands are usually best known because of their accomplishments with their ensembles. Such is not always the case, however. Billy Eckstine, for example, is better known for his fine vocalizing than for the band he led. Likewise, jazz legend Benny Carter is better known for his performance on several instruments— alto and tenor saxophone, trumpet, clarinet, trombone, and piano— and for his outstanding arranging skills than for leading the Benny Carter Orchestra.

He is also remembered for his longevity, for he was still musically active in the early 1990s, when he was well into his eighties. Born Bennett Lester Carter in New York City in 1907, he maintained artistic vigor far beyond normal expectations. He even did some composing and arranging as late as 1988, creating a new work, *Central City Sketches.* That work, recorded with the American Jazz Orchestra, with Carter conducting and playing the alto saxophone and trumpet, was a pastiche of mostly earlier works by him. Also included was "Sleep," originally the Christmas carol "Sleep, My Little Jesus," by Philadelphia musician Adam Geibel (1855-1933), who also created a variant, nondominant tune for the hymn "Stand Up, Stand Up for Jesus."

The insertion of a tender lullaby into a jazz work may seem incongruous, but that action fit the highly creative nature of Carter. With "Sleep" were several pieces by Carter, including two versions of "Doozy" and single versions of "A Kiss from You," "Central City Sketches," "Lonesome Nights," "Easy Money," "Symphony in Riffs," "Souvenir," "Blues in My Heart," and "When the Lights Are Low." The last two were written with noted songwriters: "Blues in My Heart" (1931) with Irving Mills and "When the Lights Are Low" (1936) with Spencer Williams (1889-1965). "When the Lights Are Low" is also known as "When Lights Are Low," which is also the title of a 1923 piece by Gus Kahn, Ted Koehler, and Ted

Fiorito, also songwriters of note. For whatever reason, Carter did not include in *Central City* another earlier work he wrote with two other notable songwriters, Don Raye and Gene DePaul. Perhaps he just thought that "Cow-Cow Boogie" (1942) just did not fit in with sleep and low lights.

BILLY STRAYHORN
(THE BILLY STRAYHORN ORCHESTRA, VARIOUS RECORDING DATES)

Lush Life

William Thomas "Billy" Strayhorn (1915-1967) did lead various large ensembles that could be collectively called the Billy Strayhorn Orchestra, as well as a trio, "Ellington Indigos." However, Strayhorn, a pianist born in Dayton, Ohio, is much better known as a composer, arranger, and close associate of Duke Ellington than for his notable accomplishments as a bandleader. Among the lush jazz pieces created by Strayhorn was "Lush Life" (1938), magnificently recorded in 1949 by Nat King Cole.

Strayhorn's best-known composition was the classic theme of the Duke Ellington Orchestra, "Take the 'A' Train" (1941). Another excellent Strayhorn composition is "Satin Doll" (1958), words by Johnny Mercer, music by Ellington and Strayhorn. Other numbers by Strayhorn include the following: "Day Dream" (1941), words by John Latouche, music by Ellington and Strayhorn; "Chelsea Bridge" (1942), music by Strayhorn; "Something to Live For" (1939), music by Ellington and Strayhorn. Strayhorn also composed the music for the following songs: "Multi-Colored Blue" (recorded 1961); "A Flower Is a Lovesome Thing" (recorded 1961); "Passion Flower" (recorded 1961); "Feather Roll Blues" (recorded 1947); "Triple Play" (recorded 1947); "Raincheck," or "Rain Check" (recorded 1967); "The Intimacy of the Blues" (recorded 1967); "Lotus Blossom" (recorded 1967); and "Blood Count" (recorded 1967). Of these, "Day Dream" and "Feather Roll Blues" are known to have been recorded by the Billy Strayhorn Orchestra, although Strayhorn as pianist recorded a number of others with smaller ensembles. On the same 1947 recording that presented "Feather Roll" was "Solitude" (1934), words by Eddie De-Lange and Irving Mills, music by Ellington, a hit for the Albert Hibbler Orchestra.

Note the mention of flowers in three of his instrumentals. Also note the several Strayhorn compositions recorded in 1967, the last year of his life. Another work by Strayhorn recorded in 1967, created with Ellington, suggested that Strayhorn was perhaps starting to advance to more extended and expansive pieces than his short jazz jewels. *Far East Suite,* recorded by Ellington, included "Tourist Point of View," "Bluebird of Delhi," "Isfahan," "Depk," "Mount Harissa," "Blue Pepper (Far East of the Blues)," "Agra," "Amad," and "Ad Lib on Nippon." Strayhorn and Ellington inserted an Asian flavor in this late-in-life suite, reflecting the increasingly international status of the jazz mode to which they contributed so substantially.

DON REDMAN
(THE DON REDMAN ORCHESTRA, 1931-1940)

Chant of the Weed

Because Don Redman (1900-1964) played the alto saxophone, the clarinet, and other reed instruments, his "Chant of the Weed" (1932) could just as easily have been named "the chant of the reed." What kind of weed the song referred to is uncertain, but marijuana is one possible answer. Redman's introduction of "Reefer Man" (1932), by lyricist Andy Razaf and composer J. Russel Robinson, the same year is suggestive that pot was indeed the weed in question. In any case, the Don Redman Orchestra recorded "Chant" in 1932 and adopted it as its theme. Harlan Lattimore and his Connie's Inn Orchestra also recorded "Chant" the same year.

The Redman ensemble, one of the better groups of the time, also recorded the following numbers in New York City in 1932 or 1933: "I Got the South in My Soul," more commonly known as "Got the South in My Soul" (1932), by vocalist Lee Wiley, bandleader Victor Young, and Ned Washington, who was to become an outstanding lyricist; "Underneath the Harlem Moon" (1932), by Mack Gordon and Harry Revel; "Bandana Babies" (1928), words by Dorothy Fields, music by Jimmy McHugh; "Puddin' Head Jones" (1933), by Alfred Bryan and Lou Handman; "Our Big Love Scene" (1933) and "After Sundown" (1933), both by lyricist Arthur Freed and musician Nacio Herb Brown; and "Tired of It All" and "Keep on Doin'

What You're Doin'," both by lyricist Bert Kalmar and musician Harry Ruby.

The last two songs, both recorded in 1933 and modest hits in 1934, seem to be contradictory despite having the same composers and same time frame. The very last number mentioned, "Keep on Doin' What You're Doin'," which was the final piece on a 1974 retrospective recording of music by the Redman ensemble, could be described as a combination tribute and encouraging comment to Redman, who kept on going as a bandleader and arranger for years.

Cherry

One of the first outstanding big band arrangers was Don Redman. Born in Piedmont, West Virginia, Redman learned the alto saxophone and most of the wind instruments. In 1924, he joined the Fletcher Henderson Orchestra as a performer and, ultimately, an arranger. Developing a much-copied arranging style that preserved a sense of spontaneity, used compelling call-and-response techniques with the reed and brass instruments, and enhanced solo performances, Redman over the years worked for Count Basie, Jimmie Lunceford, Harry James, Jimmy Dorsey, and others.

He also helped direct the career of Pearl Bailey for a few years and worked with (and was inspired by) Louis Armstrong when both were with Henderson. In 1927, he became the leader of McKinney's Cotton Pickers, and four years later started his own band. While directing the Cotton Pickers, he wrote one of his top numbers, "Cherry" (1928), with Redman producing the music and co-authoring the lyrics with Ray Gilbert. In a sense, then, the Cotton Pickers also became cherry pickers. After he had formed the Don Redman Orchestra, he wrote "How'm I Doin'? (Hey, Hey!)" (1932), with Lem Fowler. The answer to that question is easy, for Redman was doing very well by that time.

Hitting his peak around 1932, Redman wrote another of his top favorites, "Chant of the Weed" (1932), and his orchestra introduced "Reefer Man" (1932, words by Andy Razaf, music by J. Russel Robinson) in that year. Redman's "Chant" and "How'm I Doin'?" were recorded by other African-American orchestras in or around 1932, a most notable year for big bands. For instance, Harlan Lattimore and his Connie's Inn Orchestra recorded "Got the South in My Soul" (1932), by Lee Wiley, Ned Washington, and Victor Young, and the Claude Hopkins Orchestra recorded the orchestra's theme, "I Would Do Anything for You," or "Anything For You" (1932), by Alexander Hill, Bob Williams, and Hopkins. Also recording about the same time were the Jimmy Johnson Orchestra and King Carter and his Royal Orchestra. Add to these the white Victor Young Orchestra, which introduced "South in My Soul," and others not mentioned here, and you get an abundance of groups producing an abundance of good music.

FLETCHER HENDERSON (THE FLETCHER HENDERSON ORCHESTRA, 1924-1939, INTERMITTENTLY THEREAFTER UNTIL 1948)

Christopher Columbus

Christopher Columbus was a very famous adventurer and geographical pioneer in the late fifteenth century. Andy Razaf (1895-1973) was also, to some degree, an artistic adventurer and pioneer in the 1920s, 1930s, and 1940s. Razaf, an African-American lyricist, contributed to a number of good songs that found favor among whites as well as blacks.

In 1936, Razaf wrote the words for "Christopher Columbus" to go with a swinging melody by Leon Berry. That composition along with "Dinah" (1924, words by Sam M. Lewis and Joe Young, music by Harry Akst) were perhaps the favorite numbers of the Fletcher Henderson Orchestra, with "Christopher" serving as the band's theme. Razaf also wrote the lyrics for the classics "In the Mood" (1939, music by Joe Garland), a top favorite of the Glenn Miller Orchestra, and "Ain't Misbehavin'" (1929, music by Thomas "Fats" Waller and Harry Brooks), the theme of the Fats Waller Orchestra. He also wrote after-the-music lyrics for two other well-known pieces, "Twelfth Street Rag" (1914, music by Euday L.

Bowman) and "Stompin' at the Savoy" (1936, music by Benny Goodman, Chick Webb, and Edgar Sampson). "Stompin'" was a favorite of both the Benny Goodman Orchestra and the Chick Webb Orchestra.

Razaf also collaborated on the following numbers: the standard "Honeysuckle Rose" (1929), one of the themes of the Coleman Hawkins Orchestra, with Waller; "Blue Turning Grey Over You" (1937), with Waller; "Keepin' Out of Mischief Now" (1932), with Waller; "What Did I Do to Be So Black and Blue?" (1929), with Waller and Brooks; "The Joint Is Jumpin'" (1938), with Waller and J. C. Johnson; and "Dusky Stevadore" (1928), with Johnson. He also wrote the lyrics for "Memories of You" (1930), the theme of the Sonny Dunham Orchestra and the Memo Bernabei Orchestra, to accompany a melody by Eubie Blake. In addition, he collaborated with Paul Denniker and Michael Stoner on the excellent, but now mostly forgotten, big band number "It's Make Believe Ballroom Time" (1936), also known as "Make Believe Ballroom," which was used before, during, and after World War II as the theme of "Make Believe Ballroom" on WNEW in New York City, although in a modified form. Furthermore, he wrote "That's What I Like About the South" (1944), by himself.

The last song was the theme of the Phil Harris Orchestra. Harris is best known as a member of the cast of the Jack Benny Show, and Benny, in the mold of Columbus and Razaf, was a pioneering radio and television comedian. Fletcher Henderson was also a bit of a pioneer, leading one of the first successful African-American bands and providing a big band jazz style that set a standard for later groups.

Henderson Stomp

"Henderson Stomp," although not a jazz or big band classic, was created by a jazz and big band legend, Fletcher Henderson. Born in Cuthbert, Georgia, Henderson (1897-1952) obtained a degree in chemistry at Atlanta State University, and after moving to New York City in 1920 to pursue his academic studies, he accidentally drifted into the music business. A good pianist, he became a song plugger, then a record company manager, followed by becoming the head of a band that provided the music for touring vocalist Ethel Waters. In 1924 he formed or, better expressed, was elected leader of another ensemble that included future bandleader and outstanding arranger Don Redman.

The Fletcher Henderson Orchestra lasted until 1939, blessed by good music, top players, good arrangers (including Redman and Henderson), Henderson's nice appearance and good education, but cursed by Henderson's overly easygoing, unbusinesslike, and unambitious attitude after a relatively minor 1928 auto accident. At first a soft-style popular dance band in the mold of the Paul Whiteman Orchestra, earning Henderson the complimentary label "the colored Paul Whitman," the Henderson ensemble soon changed over to a top jazz group after Louis Armstrong joined its ranks for about a year late in 1924 or early in 1925.

In addition to being the leader of a very notable band, an arranger for his own band, an arranger for the Benny Goodman Orchestra and others during the 1940s, and a pianist for Goodman, Henderson was a competent, though not great, composer. The aforementioned "Henderson Stomp" (1927) is possibly the most noteworthy because it bore the composer's name and it was created when Henderson was approaching his zenith (which came in the early 1930s). Earlier, while with Waters, Henderson, Waters, and Alberta Hunter wrote "Down South Blues" (1923). The same year, using the name Fletcher Henderson Jr., he wrote another blues song, "I Need You to

Drive My Blues Away," with Lena Wilson. (Published with that piece was yet another 1923 blues composition, "Midnight Blues," by Babe Thompson and Spencer Williams.) In 1934, he perhaps reflected possible declining interest in his band when he created "Wrappin' It Up." After his band broke up, he collaborated on "Down South Camp Meetin'" (1943), with the noted songwriter Irving Mills. In the twenty years that passed between his "Down South Blues" and his "Down South Camp Meetin'," he seems to have gone from jazz themes to a religious one.

GUS ARNHEIM
(THE GUS ARNHEIM ORCHESTRA,
LATE 1920s-EARLY 1940s)

Sweet and Lovely

Gus Arnheim (1897-1955), born in Philadelphia, was a pianist, composer, and bandleader who is little remembered today in spite of significant associations with Stan Kenton, Woody Herman, Bing Crosby, and Fred MacMurray, a saxophonist who later turned to movie acting. All of these famous entertainers worked with the Gus Arnheim Orchestra in the 1920s or 1930s when it was a top ensemble on the West Coast.

Arnheim's compositions, although popular at the time, also have suffered the same fate of semianonymity as his orchestra. Among his songs were "Sweet and Lovely," written in 1931 by Arnheim, Harry Tobias, and Jules Lemare; "It Must Be True (You Are Mine, All Mine)" (1930), words by Arnheim and Gordon Clifford, music by Harry Barris; "Mandalay" (1924), by Earl Burnett, Arnheim, and Abe Lyman; and "I Cried for You" (1923), by Arnheim, Lyman, and Arthur Freed. "Sweet and Lovely," "It Must Be True," and "I Cried for You" were all themes of Arnheim.

The previous list of songwriters includes three musicians of some notoriety. Barris wrote the very popular novelty "Mississippi Mud" in 1927 and "Wrap Your Troubles in Dreams" in 1931, with Ted Koehler and Billy Moll. (It is interesting to note that what one did with one's troubles changed over the sixteen years since lyricist

George Asaf and composer Felix Powell created their World War I era smash "Pack Up Your Troubles in Your Old Kit Bag and Smile, Smile, Smile" [1915].) "Wrap Your Troubles," recorded by Bing Crosby with the Arnheim Orchestra, helped propel the young singer to vocal stardom. Lyman, a drummer, had his own orchestra, in which Arnheim was a pianist. (Lyman's top numbers included the two songs by him mentioned previously and his theme, "California, Here I Come" [1924], lyrics by Al Jolson and Bud DeSylva, music by Joseph Meyer.) Freed was a movie producer and a noted song lyricist who worked with composer Nacio Herb Brown to produce enduring songs such as "Singin' in the Rain" (1929) and "Temptation" (1933). The 1933 composition helped make Crosby a film star when he crooned the piece in *Going Hollywood*. In short, Arnheim was an accomplished, but relatively obscure, musician surrounded by a sea of better-known personalities.

Them There Eyes

"Them There Eyes," a charming and quite successful swing era number, was a favorite of the Gus Arnheim Orchestra. Yet the composition, created in 1930 by Maceo Pinkard, Doris Tauber, and William Tracey, is not heard much today. The same could be said about the other songs of the threesome, with one exception.

Pinkard, Ben Bernie, and Kenneth Casey collaborated on the 1925 jazz classic "Sweet Georgia Brown." Otherwise, Pinkard, Tauber, and Tracey have been relegated to historical footnotes, although they all produced other pieces that had at least a bit of success. Pinkard cowrote the slightly enduring "Gimme a Little Kiss, Will Ya, Huh?" (1926), with Roy Turk and Jack Smith, and "Sugar" (1927), a favorite of the Count Basie Orchestra, with Sidney D. Mitchell. He also wrote "Congratulations" (1929), with Coleman Goetz, Bud Green, and Sam H. Stept; "Here Comes the Showboat" (1927), words by Billy Rose, music by Pinkard; "Jazz Baby's Ball" (1920), words by Charles Bayha, music by Pinkard; and "Mammy O' Mine" (1919), words by Tracey, music by Pinkard. Tauber also collaborated with Mann Curtis on "Fooled" (1955). Tracey also wrote a number of mostly forgotten songs.

Pinkard was an associate of Ben Bernie (best-known for his leadership of the Ben Bernie Orchestra); he cowrote top numbers for the very good, but underappreciated, Gus Arnheim Orchestra and the very good and famous Count Basie Orchestra, plus a jazz blockbuster. Although he helped write compositions with "sweet," "sugar," "congratulations," and "showboat" in the titles, his historical fate has been better reflected by the title of one of his collaborators' works, "Fooled."

JEAN GOLDKETTE
(THE JEAN GOLDKETTE ORCHESTRA, 1924-1929, VARIOUS-SIZED GROUPS OCCASIONALLY INTO EARLY 1950s)

Remember

A number of foreign-born musicians found considerable success as bandleaders in the United States, including Ray Noble, Ted Heath, Desi Arnaz, Xavier Cugat, Jan Savitt, Charlie Spivak, and Jean Goldkette. Of these several notable leaders, Jean Goldkette (1899-1962), born in Valenciennes, France, is probably the least known to the general public. A child prodigy concert pianist with a love for classical music, Goldkette came to America at the age of twelve. Not long after arriving in the United States, he began work as a dance band pianist for one of the several Edgar Benson orchestras.

In time, Goldkette became director of a Benson ensemble and eventually formed over twenty of his own bands, all under the umbrella heading of the Jean Goldkette Orchestra. His various groups performed successfully from the mid-1920s to the 1950s. The following were among the top numbers of Goldkette: "Remember" (1925), a fine, gentle, nostalgic piece by the great Irving Berlin (1888-1989), who also wrote the 1911 classic "Alexander's Ragtime Band," the theme of the Van Alexander Orchestra; "Clementine," or "My Darling Clementine" (1884), an American western-style favorite of uncertain authorship; "Dinah" (1924), a standard ballad by lyricists Sam M. Lewis and Joe Young and musician Harry Akst; Goldkette's themes "I Know That You Know" (1926), words by Anne Caldwell, music by Vincent Youmans, and "Sweetheart Time" (1915), words by Harold A. Robe, music by Milbury H. Ryder ("Sweetheart" was also a theme of the Paul Specht Orchestra); and the relatively obscure "My Blackbirds Are Bluebirds Now" (1928), by Irving Caesar and Cliff Friend.

Also recorded by Goldkette were "(What Can I Say) After I Say I'm Sorry?" (1926), by Walter Donaldson and Abe Lyman; "Lonesome and Sorry" (1926), by Benny Davis and Con Conrad; "Here Comes the Showboat" (1927), words by Billy Rose, music by Maceo Pinkard; and "She's Funny That Way" (1920), words by Richard A. Whiting, music by Neil Moret. (Whiting also wrote the music for "Hooray for Hollywood" [1938], the theme of the Johnny "Scat" Davis Orchestra, words by Johnny Mercer.) All of the aforementioned numbers, except "Hooray for Hollywood," were recorded in the period from 1924 to 1929, when the Goldkette Orchestras were at their peak. After that, his musical enterprises gradually declined, but Goldkette gathered a lot of gold. More of an astute entrepreneur than a hands-on musician (he never played in any of the later bands), his career could be summed up by "big band, big bank, little remembered."

Tip Toe Through the Tulips

Jean Goldkette, similar to other directors of big bands, sometimes performed novelty or goofy numbers to attract audiences. One of the favorite numbers of the Jean Goldkette Orchestra was "Tiptoe Through the Tulips," or "Tip Toe Through the Tulips" (1929). In addition to being a goofy piece with all of the four or five (take your choice) words in the title starting with "T," it was a favorite of the goofy and childlike entertainer of 1960s and 1970s fame, "Tiny Tim" (two more Ts!). Another variant of the title, the more official one, "Tip Toe Through the Tulips with Me," gets away from the litany of Ts, as do all of the letters of the names of the song's creators, Al Dubin (1891-1945), who wrote the words, and Joseph A. Burke (1884-1950), who wrote the music.

Two other songs with goofy, or at least catchy, titles recorded by Goldkette were "Where the Lazy Daisies Grow" (1924), by Cliff Friend, and "My Blackbirds Are Bluebirds Now" (1928), by Friend and Irving Caesar. The latter song was recorded by Goldkette in at least two different versions in 1929 and was one of the numbers included in a 1985 anthology of the Goldkette orchestra, Les Brown and his Band of Renown, and the Richard Himber Orchestra.

Himber's ensemble is possibly even less famous than Goldkette's unappreciated group. Probably the best-known work associated with Himber is his theme song, "It Isn't Fair" (1933), words by Himber, music by Himber, Frank Warshauer, and Sylvester Sprigato. Despite the occasional playing of that song toward the end of the century, Himber, similar to Goldkette, is relatively obscure today. Is that fair?

JOHN SCOTT TROTTER
(THE JOHN SCOTT TROTTER
ORCHESTRA, VARIOUS STUDIO
RECORDINGS, LATE 1930s-LATE 1960s)

Swinging on a Star

John Scott Trotter is one of those familiar yet fuzzy names from the past. Born in Charlotte, North Carolina, pianist Trotter (1908-1975) became a top arranger, settling in Hollywood around 1936. He did a lot of recording during the late 1930s and 1940s, including being the music director for the legendary vocalist Bing Crosby. He remained active until at least the late 1960s, when he was the music director for the film *A Boy Named Charlie Brown* (1969). Vince Guaraldi wrote the music and Rod McKuen the lyrics for that charming movie featuring the *Peanuts* characters.

The John Scott Trotter Orchestra produced so many records that it could be described as more of a galloping than a trotting group. Perhaps his most notable rendition was the Crosby favorite "Swinging on a Star" (1944), words by Johnny Burke (1908-1964), music by James "Jimmy" Van Heusen (1913-1990), which won an Academy Award for its use in the film *Going My Way*. Burke also was co-author of "Scatterbrain" (1939), one of the themes of the Frankie Masters Orchestra, with Masters, Kahn Keene, and Carl Bean. However, the other Masters theme, "Moonlight and You" (1924), was written by an earlier songwriting group, Art Sizemore, Dan

Russo, and John Alden. Burke and Van Heusen also collaborated on "Blue Rain" (1939), one of the themes of the Alvino Rey Orchestra. Another theme of Rey was "Nightie-Night" (1925), words by Ira Gershwin, music by George Gershwin. The Gershwins also wrote one of the themes of the Paul Specht Orchestra, "Evening Star" (1924). The other Specht theme, "Sweetheart Time" (1915), also a theme of the Jean Goldkette Orchestra, was by lyricist Harold A. Robe and composer Milbury H. Ryder.

The Trotter orchestra also swung on the star of Crosby when it accompanied the singer for another notable recording, "Blue Skies" (1927), by Irving Berlin, for the 1946 film of that name.

Among the numerous other recordings by Trotter from the late 1930s to the 1960s, often with Crosby, were the following: "All of My Life" (1945), by Berlin; "An Apple for the Teacher" (1939), by Burke and James V. Monaco; "The Bells of St. Mary's" (1917), words by Douglas Furber, music by A. Emmett Adams; "Between Eighteenth and Nineteenth on Chestnut Street" (1940), by Dick Rogers and Will Osborne (Osborne and Paul Denniker cowrote the theme of the Will Osborne Orchestra, "Beside an Open Fireplace" [1929]); "Bob White" (1937), words by Johnny Mercer, music by Bernard Hanighan; "But Beautiful" (1947), words by Burke, music by Van Heusen; "Can't Get Indiana Off My Mind" (1940), by Robert DeLeon and Hoagy Carmichael; "Close As Pages in a Book" (1945), words by Dorothy Fields, music by Sigmund Romberg; "Dearly Beloved" (1942), words by Mercer, music by Jerome Kern; "East Side of Heaven" (1939), words by Burke, music by Monaco; "A Fella with an Umbrella" (1948), by Berlin; "(Just Say I'm a) Friend of Yours" (1945), words by Burke, music by Van Heusen; "A Gal in Calico" (1947), words by Leo Robin, music by Arthur Schwartz; "(It's Just the) Gypsy in My Soul" (1937), words by Moe Jaffe and Clay Boland, music by Boland; "Imagination" (1940) and "It Could Happen to You" (1944), both with words by Burke and music by Van Heusen; "I Do, Do, Do Like You" (1947), by Allie Wrubel; "I Don't Want to Walk Without You" (1941), words by Frank Loesser, music by Jule Styne; and "June Comes Around Once Every Year" (1945), words by Mercer, music by Harold Arlen (who also wrote the music for "I Gotta Right to Sing the Blues" [1932], the theme of the Jack Teagarden Orchestra, with lyrics by Ted Koehler).

We will continue to take the long way home by mentioning more and more songs that may seem to go on forever: "Let's Take the Long Way Home" (1944), words by Mercer, music by Arlen; "The Moon Got in My Eyes" (1937), words by Burke, music by Arthur Johnston; "More and More" (1944), words by Edgar Yipsel Harburg, music by Kern; "Only Forever" (1940), words by Burke, music by Monaco; "Out of This World" (1945), words by Mercer, music by Arlen; "Pale Moon" (1920), words by Jesse Glick, music by Frederic Knight Logan; "Personality" (1946), words by Burke, music by Van Heusen; "Pocketful of Dreams" (1938), words by Burke, music by Monaco; "Skylark" (1941), words by Mercer, music by Carmichael; "These Foolish Things" (1936), words by Holt Marvell, music by Jack Strachey and Harry Link; "Too-Ra-Loo-Ra-Loo-Rah" (1914), by James Royce Shannon; "Tumbling Tumbleweeds" (1934), by Bob Nolan; "When Irish Eyes Are Smiling" (1912), words by Chauncy Olcott and George Graff Jr., music by Ernest R. Ball; and "You Ain't Heard Nothing Yet" (1919), by Al Jolson, Gus Kahn, and Bud DeSylva. DeSylva, colyricist Lew Brown, and musician Ray Henderson collaborated on the theme of the Johnny Catron Orchestra, "Just a Memory" (1927). Henderson in turn collaborated with lyricists Billy Rose and Mort Dixon on the theme of the Benny Strong Orchestra, "That Old Gang of Mine" (1923), and Dixon was involved with another theme, that of the Roger Wolfe Kahn Orchestra, the 1927 "Where the Wild, Wild Flowers Grow," words by Dixon, melody by Harry Woods. Getting toward the end of the alphabet and the end of this recitation, we should also mention the fine composition "Yours Is My Heart Alone" (1931), German lyrics ("Dein ist mein ganzes Herz") by Ludwig Herzer and Fritz Lohner, English lyrics by Harry B. Smith, music by Franz Lehár, extracted from Lehár's 1923 operetta *Die gelbe Jacke*.

From the "a" in "All of My Life" to the "z" in "Herz," the previous only partial listing is sort of a summary of the musical life of John Scott Trotter, a productive but not well-known bandleader.

MAL HALLETT
(THE MAL HALLETT ORCHESTRA, MID-1920s–MID-1940s)

Good-Night, My Love

Mal Hallett (1893-1952), an alto sax player born in Roxbury, Massachusetts, led a good, but not famous, big band. The Mal Hallett Orchestra was perhaps at its peak when it recorded "Good-Night, My Love" in 1936. Although "Good-Night," written in 1934 by two notable songwriters, Harry Revel (1905-1958) and Mack Gordon (1904-1959), is by no means a classic, the song as recorded by Hallett was used in a significant 1936 movie musical, *Stowaway*. Also in that film was another Revel and Gordon composition recorded by Hallett, "One Never Knows, Does One?" (1936). Similar to the orchestral ensemble, the vocalist for these two recordings, Jerry Perkins, is not well known.

Other decades are also represented in recordings by the Hallett ensemble. Two early-in-the-century pieces, "Down by the Old Mill Stream," the barbershop favorite created in 1910 by Tell Taylor, and "St. Louis Blues," the jazz classic written in 1914 by W. C. Handy, were recorded by Hallett. Songs from the 1940s favored by Hallett included "Long Ago and Far Away" (1944), the dreamy ballad by lyricist Ira Gershwin and composer Jerome Kern; lively "G. I. Jive" (1943), by another outstanding popular songwriter, Johnny Mercer; and "When They Ask About You" (1943), by lesser-known Sam H. Stept.

Reviewing the previous five songs that first appeared during the tenure of the Hallett orchestra—"Good-Night," "One Never Knows," "Long Ago," "G. I.," and "When They Ask"—one is reminded of the old chicken-versus-egg debate. None of the five songs is well known today or very enduring, although "Long Ago" and "G. I." are still remembered to some extent. Does the lack of staying power of these songs result from the Mal Hallett Orchestra being far from famous, or is Hallett less known because of the modest successes of his favored numbers? Adding fuel to the inquiry is the fact that another lesser-known ensemble, the Paul Weston Orchestra, also recorded "Long Ago" and "G. I."

In the Chapel in the Moonlight

Short-lived Billy Hill (1899-1940) is not a famous songwriter, but he did produce some noteworthy songs in his final years. One of these was "In the Chapel in the Moonlight" (1936), a favorite of the Mal Hallett Orchestra. The following were other songs of consequence by Hill: "The Last Round-Up" (1933); "The Old Spinning Wheel" (1933); "Wagon Wheels" (1934), words by Hill, music by Peter DeRose, based on William Arms Fisher's "Goin' Home" (1922), which in turn was derived from the second movement of Antonin Dvořák's *New World Symphony* (1893); "Alone at a Table for Two" (1935), words by Hill and Daniel Richman, music by Ted Fiorito; "Empty Saddles" (1936); "The Glory of Love" (1936); "Lights Out" (1936); "The Call of the Canyon" (1940); and "On a Little Street in Singapore" (1940), words and music by Hill and DeRose. With compositions about round-ups, wagon wheels, saddles, and canyons, Hill definitely leaned toward western songs. However, he did not lean too heavily toward fame, for only "Wagon Wheels" and "The Glory of Love," with its memorable lines "That's the story of, that's the glory of, love," have not been ravaged too much by time and taste.

Other songs, in addition to "In the Chapel," that were favored by Hallett included "Ridin' High" and "Boo Hoo." Active "Ridin' High" was written by Cole Porter for the 1936 Broadway musical *Red Hot and Blue!* and recorded in 1937 by Hallett, along with a future bandleader, Frankie Carle. Pseudosad "Boo Hoo" (1937), also a favorite of Guy Lombardo and his Royal Canadians, was written in 1937 by Edward Heyman, John Jacob Loeb, and Guy's brother, Carmen Lombardo. Since Hallett never achieved a lot of fame, any hopes of "Ridin' High" ended up with a bit of "Boo Hoo."

MITCHELL AYRES
(MITCHELL AYRES
AND HIS FASHIONS IN MUSIC,
MID-1930s–MID-1940s)

I'll Remember April

Mitchell Ayres and his Fashions in Music were a somewhat successful band who made a number of recordings in the late 1930s and early 1940s, as well as appearing live and in films. Led by Mitchell Ayres (1910-1959), a violinist from Milwaukee, the group had no really big hits. Ayres changed his original surname, Agress, to the more musically compatible Ayres, which perhaps deliberately was reminiscent of the musical term "airs."

The theme song of Ayres the bandleader was "You Go to My Head" (1938), words by Haven Gillespie, music by J. Fred Coots, a far from dizzying success. Of somewhat more impact were Ayres's recordings of the long-titled "Everybody Loves My Baby, but My Baby Don't Love Nobody but Me" (1924) and the sentimental "I'll Remember April" (1942). "Everybody Loves" was created by two fairly significant songwriters, Jack Palmer and Spencer Williams. Palmer also collaborated with Cab Calloway on a Calloway jazz favorite, "Jumpin' Jive" (1939). Williams also wrote two top jazz numbers, "Royal Garden Blues" (1919, with Clarence Williams), a favorite of the Tommy Dorsey Orchestra, and "Basin Street Blues" (1929), perhaps a classic.

"I'll Remember April," also known as "I Remember April," was by a modestly successful songwriting team, Don Raye and Gene DePaul, along with Patricia Johnston. Although April may be remembered, the only one of that trio who is remembered to much extent is Raye (1909-   ), who created the World War II hit "Boogie Woogie Bugle Boy (from Company B)" (1941, with Hughie Prince) and the undervalued patriotic choral favorite "This Is My Country" (1940, with Al Jacobs). Much more memorable is Ella Fitzgerald's rendition of "A-Tisket, A-Tasket," which she and Al Feldman adapted in 1938 from the nursery rhyme that first appeared about 1879. She lovingly nursed the lively novelty while riding on a bus in a scene from the 1942 Abbott and Costello comedy movie *Ride 'em Cowboy,* which also featured "I'll Remember April."

Unfortunately, in spite of their fine association with "Everybody" and "April," Mitchell Ayres and his Fashions in Music did not play enough fashionable numbers in a fashionable enough style to make it to the big time in the big band era.

NEAL HEFTI
(THE NEAL HEFTI ORCHESTRA, OCCASIONAL LIVE PERFORMANCES AND RECORDINGS, MOSTLY IN THE MID-1950s–LATE 1960s)

Batman Theme

Yes, readers, there was a Neal Hefti before Batman. Born in Hastings, Nebraska, in 1922, Hefti became a trumpet player in the Charlie Barnet Orchestra in 1942 and in the Woody Herman Orchestra in 1944. While with Herman he wrote two instrumentals, "The Good Earth" (1944) and "Wild Root" (1946, with Herman), which Herman turned into hit recordings. As time went on, his arrangement work, which had begun in the late 1930s and started to expand into original compositions in the 1940s, became more and more important. In the late 1940s, he wrote arrangements for the Harry James Orchestra. In the mid-1950s, he helped the Count Basie Orchestra change to a more precise, more disciplined, and crisper new style. Overall, he was one of the more significant big band arrangers around midcentury, bringing more order and system to the art of jazz band arrangement.

During the 1950s and 1960s, he wrote a fair amount of original music for films and television. This period of composition culminated in the hard-hitting and highly successful theme (including lyrics) for the series *Batman* (1966) and the light and bouncy theme for the film and later television series *The Odd Couple* (1968). (Sammy Cahn wrote the lyrics for the show's theme.) None of Hefti's compositions, except the aforementioned two, are particularly well known, and most of them have titles as concise and efficient as Hefti's arrangement style was precise and disciplined. The various big bands formed by Hefti were likewise not of long duration, periodically serving to perform concerts live or to record the music of Hefti and others. Whereas other bandleaders headed multiple bands because of artistic, financial, or personal changes in their lives, Hefti led multiple ensembles by plan.

Among the numbers performed by the various manifestations of the Neal Hefti Orchestra, in addition to "Batman" and "The Odd Couple," were the following pieces by Hefti: "Splanky" (1958); "Li'l Darling" (1959); "Cherry Point" (1963); "Coral Reef" (1963), Hefti's theme song; "Cute" (1963); "Plymouth Rock" (1964); "Sure Thing" (1964); "Why Not" (1964); "Barefoot in the Park" (1967), for the 1967 film of the same name; and "The Kid from Red Bank" (date uncertain, possibly around 1980). Like most of Hefti's titles, we will be short and to the point and end this essay.

PAUL WESTON
(THE PAUL WESTON ORCHESTRA,
VARIOUS STUDIO RECORDINGS
1940s-1970s)

G. I. Jive

In the midst of World War II, when there were many GIs and a lot of jive in the music world, the song "G. I. Jive" (1943) came onto the American scene. Written by world-famous lyricist and composer Johnny Mercer (1909-1976), who was born in Savannah, Georgia, "G. I. Jive" was a hit during the conflict but was almost forgotten after peace finally arrived. (Donald Kahn has also been mentioned as Mercer's collaborator on "Jive.") Louis Jordan and his Tympany Five recorded "Jive," as did the Paul Weston Orchestra.

Weston (1912-), a pianist, composer, and bandleader born Paul Wetstein in Pittsfield, or according to some sources, Springfield, Massachusetts, is also known as Paul Wetstein and has used the pseudonym Jonathan Edwards. He also recorded the Bing Crosby favorite "Ac-cent-tchuate the Positive" (1944), words by Mercer, music by Harold Arlen. (Mercer and Arlen also collaborated on the Frank Sinatra favorite "One for My Baby [and One More for the Road]" one year earlier.) Weston, in addition, recorded another notable number by another notable songwriting team, "Long Ago and Far Away" (1944). Lyricist Ira Gershwin and composer Jerome

Kern wrote dreamy "Long Ago," which might have become a classic, or at least a standard, except for the somewhat hard-to-master tempo of the notes accompanying the phrase "long ago." Weston and vocalist Jo Stafford made a fine rendition of it in 1944, but that wasn't enough to overcome the subtle flaw.

Weston also wrote several songs. With yet another renowned lyricist, Sammy Cahn, plus Axel Stordahl, he created "I Should Care" (1945) and "Day by Day" (1946). (The latter should not be confused with the popular "Day by Day" from Stephen Schwartz's 1971 rock musical *Godspell*.) Weston and Cahn also collaborated on "Autumn in Rome" (1954), and Weston and Paul Mason Howard coproduced "Shrimp Boats" (1951) and "The Gandy Dancers' Ball" (1952). "Shrimp" and "Gandy," both active numbers, possibly reflected Weston's delight at making contributions without being in the shadows of better-known artists such as Mercer, Crosby, Arlen, Gershwin, Kern, and Cahn.

RAY NOBLE
(THE RAY NOBLE ORCHESTRA, 1935-1938)

Goodnight, Sweetheart

Well over a dozen popular songs begin with "Good Night" and/or "Goodnight," including the following: "Good Night" (1968), by John Lennon and Paul McCartney; "Good Night, Angel" (1937), words by Herb Magidson, music by Allie Wrubel; "Good Night, Nurse" (1912), words by Thomas J. Gray, music by Raymond Walker; "Goodnight, Irene" (1936), by Huddie Ledbetter; "Goodnight, My Love" (1934), words by Mack Gordon, music by Harry Revel; "Goodnight, My Someone" (1957), by Meredith Willson; "Goodnight, Ladies" (1847), words by E. P. Christy, music anonymous; and another "Goodnight, Ladies" (1911), words by Harry H. Williams, music by Egbert Van Alstyne. Some, perhaps all, of these titles can be found under both "Good Night" or "Goodnight."

One of the most famous "goodnight" compositions is "Goodnight, Sweetheart" (1931), by Ray Noble (1903-1978), James Campbell, and Reginald Connelly. (Just as the use of "Goodnight" in the 1931 song was far from original, it has been suggested that the melody of the piece may have been derived from "Symphony in C" by Franz Schubert and "Les Preludes" [1854] by Franz Liszt. Which of Schubert's symphonies was being referred to, however, is uncertain, for three of his symphonies, No. 4, No. 6, and No. 9, are in C.) Noble, a notable bandleader as well as significant composer, was born in Brighton, England. James or Jimmy Campbell and Reginald Connelly also wrote "Try a Little Tenderness" (1932) with Harry Woods, plus "By the Fireside" (1932), and "I Found You" (1931), both with Noble.

"Goodnight, Sweetheart" was the closing theme of the Ray Noble Orchestra as well as one of Noble's biggest hits. Other themes of Noble include "The Very Thought of You" (1934), by Noble, and "I'll See You in My Dreams" (1924), words by Gus Kahn, music by Isham Jones (also a favorite of the Isham Jones Orchestra). Other hits by the Noble ensemble, which was popular in both Great Britain and the United States, included the following: "Linda" (1947), by Jack Lawrence and Ann Ronell, one of Noble's top numbers; "Lady of Spain" (1931), words by Erell Reaves, music by Tolchard Evans; "The Old Spinning Wheel" (1933), by Billy Hill; "Isle of Capri" (1934), words by Jimmy Kennedy, music by Will Grosz; "Paris in the Spring" (1935), by Mack Gordon and Harry Revel; "Easy to Love" (1936) and "I've Got You Under My Skin" (1936), both by Cole Porter; "I'll Dance at Your Wedding" (1947), words by Herb Magidson, music by Ben Oakland; "By the Light of the Silvery Moon" (1909), words by Edward Madden, music by Gus Edwards; and a trio of winners by Irving Berlin, "I've Got My Love to Keep Me Warm" (1937), "Alexander's Ragtime Band" (1911), and "Change Partners" (1938).

Love Is the Sweetest Thing

Love can be the sweetest thing, no matter toward whom or what the passion is directed. When Ray Noble wrote "Love Is the Sweetest Thing" in 1933, however, it is not totally clear whether the object of his musical affection was an anonymous lady or his country of birth, England. The reason for such doubt is the similarity of the first five notes of "Sweetest Thing" to the first five notes of "God Save the King" (1744), the national anthem of Great Britain.

Most likely, Noble, whether consciously or unconsciously, intended the five-note borrowing to be an indirect form of homage to his homeland. In contrast, his other notable songs were clearly focused on the main topic of popular songs—romance. Some of his compositions do suggest romance, for example, "Why the Stars Come Out Tonight" (1936); "Love Locked Out" (1933), words by Max Kester, music by Noble; "Brighter Than the Sun" (1932); "Cherokee" (1939); "By the Fireside" (1932), with James Campbell and Reginald Connelly; and "Goodnight, Sweetheart" (1931), with Campbell and Connelly. Noble also created several pieces with "you" or "your" clearly in the titles. These unequivocally romantic songs are "I Found You" (1931), with Campbell and Connelly; "I Hadn't Anyone Till You" (1938); "I'll Be Good Because of You" (1931), with Alan Murray; "The Touch of Your Lips" (1936); and the excellent "The Very Thought of You" (1934), which was one of his biggest favorites as well as one of his theme songs.

Noble, who left England in 1934, was a celebrity in the United States in the 1930s, 1940s, and 1950s. He appeared with George Burns and Gracie Allen on radio and with Edgar Bergen on television, in addition to writing hit songs and leading a successful band. However, neither Noble nor the Ray Noble Orchestra is well remembered by the general public, especially its younger members.

SY OLIVER
(THE SY OLIVER ORCHESTRA, VARIOUS TIMES FROM 1947–MID-1950s)

Yes, Indeed

Yes, indeed, Sy Oliver was an important figure in the development of jazz and the big bands. Although not very well known to the general public, Oliver (1910-1988), born Melvin James Oliver in Battle Creek, Michigan, was a trumpet player, bandleader, composer, and arranger. After playing with several bands, including the outstanding Jimmie Lunceford Orchestra, he formed two artistically excellent, but commercially unsuccessful, groups of his own.

The Sy Oliver Orchestra did not fail to become a big-name ensemble because of its musical quality or technical skill, but because Oliver would not follow paths or compromises that attracted large audiences. He wrote several very good compositions, which his band used in its performances. These numbers were "Yes, Indeed" (1941), recorded by the Tommy Dorsey Orchestra in 1941, with vocals by Jo Stafford and Oliver (the piece became a hit in 1943); "Easy Does It" (1939), words by Oliver, music by Oliver and Jimmy Young, introduced by Dorsey; "Well, Git It!" (1942), music by Oliver; "For Dancers Only" (1937), words by Don Raye and Vic Schoen, music by Oliver, introduced by Jimmie Lunceford and one of the favorite numbers of the Lunceford ensemble; and, best of all, the superb swing era classic "Opus One," or "Opus Number One" (1944), music by Oliver, one of the top favorites of Tommy Dorsey.

Oliver also was a brilliant arranger, working with, among others, three of the most famous bands, those of Lunceford, Dorsey, and Benny Goodman. It was in the area of arrangement that Oliver made his greatest contributions, creating energetic, clear, crisp, yet often intricate arrangements especially notable for his handling of brass instruments. Two of his best arrangements were of "Swing High, Swing Low," a 1937 piece by lyricist Ralph Freed and composer Burton Lane, and of "On the Sunny Side of the Street," a 1930 song by lyricist Dorothy Fields and composer Jimmy McHugh. His style of arrangement was highly influential in the definition and development of big band music and was widely copied. He also, similar to Goodman, helped to bridge the gaps between black and white musicians, working well with whites such as Goodman, Dorsey, Stafford, Raye, and Schoen, all notable figures of the big band era.

VIC SCHOEN
(THE VIC SCHOEN ORCHESTRA, VARIOUS STUDIO RECORDINGS FROM LATE 1930s-1950s)

Bei Mir Bist Du Schoen

Although he was a trumpet player, an arranger with several top bands, a composer, and a bandleader, Vic Schoen, born Victor Schoen in Brooklyn, New York, is scarcely known among the American public. Schoen (1916-) is perhaps best viewed by tracking the activities of his big band. The Vic Schoen Orchestra flourished during the late 1930s, the 1940s, and the early 1950s. Among the many recordings made by Schoen was a number that had his surname in the title. "Bei Mir Bist Du Schoen" was written in 1937 by wordsmith Sammy Cahn (1913-1992), originally Samuel Cohen, and by composer Saul Chaplin (1912-1997), originally Saul Kaplan. They adapted a Yiddish song they had heard in 1936, Cahn devising English lyrics and Chaplin preparing an arrangement of the melody. Soon after, the Andrews Sisters, for whom Schoen was an arranger and music director, gained considerable fame with an intimate yet swinging rendition of what would become a top big band favorite. (Cahn and Chaplin also wrote the theme of the Andy Kirk Orchestra, "[It Will Have to Do] Until the Real Thing Comes Along" (1936), with L. E. Freeman, Mann Holiner, and Alberta Nichols.)

Vic Schoen almost surely adopted "Bei Mir" as one of his top numbers because of the coincidence of the word "Schoen," which is derived from the German word "schön," meaning "beautiful." However, the bandleader probably pronounced his name differently from the way the German word sounded in the song, that is, "shane." Yet Schoen also surely recognized the considerable commercial appeal of the lively piece with the strange name whose basic sentiments are that you are grand and I love you.

The following are other 1930s or earlier numbers recorded by Schoen: "Don't Sit Under the Apple Tree" (1939), words by Lew Brown and Charles Tobias, music by Sam H. Stept, another top hit for the Andrews Sisters; "For Dancers Only" (1937), words by Don Raye and Schoen, music by Sy Oliver (Schoen's other compositions include "Amen" [1942] and "Hopeless Heart" [1949]); "Everywhere You Go" (1927), by Larry Shay and Mark Fisher; "Gonna Get a Girl" (1927), by Howard Simon and Al Lewis; "I May Be Wrong, but I Think You're Wonderful" (1929), words by Harry Ruskin, music by Henry Sullivan; "Oh, Johnny, Oh, Johnny, Oh" (1917), words by Ed Rose, music by Abe Olman; "Oh, Lady, Be Good" (1924), words by Ira Gershwin, music by George Gershwin; and "Rainbow Round My Shoulder," or "There's a Rainbow Round My Shoulder" (1928), by Al Jolson, Billy Rose, and Dave Dreyer. (Incidentally, Ed Rose and Billy Rose should not be confused with David Rose, who wrote the excellent 1944 instrumental "Holiday for Strings," the theme of the David Rose Orchestra, and who also was the first husband of great songstress Judy Garland.)

For years, the Vic Schoen Orchestra played music that at least approached the beauty and variety of a rainbow, but historically, the ensemble is about as elusive as that phenomenon in the sky.

Rum and Coca Cola

Two of the top numbers of the Vic Schoen Orchestra, "Bei Mir Bist Du Schoen" (1938) and "Rum and Coca Cola" (1945), were both borrowed hits. Lyricist Sammy Cahn and composer Saul Chaplin openly based "Bei Mir" on a Yiddish song, and "Rum and Coca Cola" (1945) also involved a lot of borrowing. The "Coca Cola" in the title was, of course, a reference to the fabulously successful soft drink, and the English lyrics by Morey Amsterdam (1912-1996) were derived from the original Spanish lyrics by Clotilde Arias. Most notable, the melody by Jeri Sullavan (1924-   ) and Paul Baron was supposedly plagiarized from "L'Année Passée" (1906), by composer Lionel Belasco. A suit brought by Belasco's publisher was decided in favor of Belasco, and "Rum and Coca Cola," though a big hit of the 1940s, became somewhat tainted goods.

Other less controversial songs from about the same period that were recorded by Schoen included the following: "Blues in the Night" (1941), words by Johnny Mercer, music by Harold Arlen (in one of the numerous arrangements by Schoen); "Ac-cent-tchuate the Positive" (1944), words by Mercer, music by Arlen; "Along the Navajo Trail" (1945), by Dick Charles, Eddie DeLange, and Larry Markes; "The Wedding Samba" (1947), by Abraham Ellstein, Allan Small, and Joseph Leibowitz; "You Don't Have to Know the Language" (1947), "But Beautiful" (1947), and "Life Is So Peculiar" (1950), all three by lyricist Johnny Burke and musician Jimmy Van Heusen; "Pennsylvania Polka" (1942), by Lester Lee and Zeke Manners; "Get Your Kicks on Route 66," or "Route 66" (1946), by Bob Troup (this piece should not be confused with the jazzy theme for the television series *Route 66,* created in 1960 by Nelson Riddle); "How It Lies, How It Lies, How It Lies" (1949), words by Paul Francis Webster, music by Sonny Burke; "I've Never Been in Love Before" (1950), by Frank Loesser; "Show Business," or "There's No Business Like Show Business" (1946), by Irving Berlin; "Huggin' and Chalkin'" (1946), by Kermit Goell and Clarence Leonard Hayes; "Near You" (1947), words by Goell, music by Francis Craig, the theme of the Francis Craig Orchestra and the Jack Crawford Orchestra; "Kiss Me Sweet" (1949), by Milton Drake; and "South America, Take It Away" (1946), by Harold Rome.

Although brief in fame and duration, the Vic Schoen Orchestra did crank out a decent number of small musical victories.

Appendix

Themes of Some Other Bands

Many big bands have not been mentioned, directly or indirectly, in the essays presented in this volume. To help make this history of the bands more complete, a list of some other ensembles and at least one of their themes is included here, along with brief historical data on the numbers listed. It should be noted that historical sources may vary as to the theme for any specific group, and that bands often changed their themes.

Al Donahue Orchestra: "Lowdown Rhythm in a Top Hat" (1939), words (w) and music (m) (w/m) Al Donahue, Terry Shand, Jimmy Eaton.

Anson Weeks Orchestra: "I'm Sorry Dear" (1931), w/m Anson Weeks, Harry Tobias, Johnnie Scott.

Art Kassell Orchestra: "Doodle-Doo-Doo" (1924), w/m Art Kassell, Mel Stitzel.

Bennie Krueger Orchestra: "It's Getting Dark on Old Broadway" (1922), w/m Louis A. Hirsch, Gene Buck, Dave Stamper.

Benny Meroff Orchestra: "Diane" (1927), w/m Erno Rapée, Lew Pollack.

Bernie Cummins and his Hotel Roosevelt Orchestra: "Dark Eyes," or "Black Eyes" (1926), traditional Russian folk song arranged by Harry Horlick, Gregory Stone.

Billy Butterfield Orchestra: "Moonlight in Vermont" (1944), w John Blackburn, m Karl Suessdorf.

Billy May Orchestra: "Lean, Baby" (1951), w/m Billy May.

Bobby Byrne Orchestra: "Danny Boy," w Frederick E. Weatherly (1913), m folk air from County Londonderry, Northern Ireland (published 1855).

Bobby Sherwood Orchestra: "The Elk's Parade," w/m Bobby Sherwood (recorded 1942).

Boyd Senter Orchestra: "Bad Habits" (recorded 1927), w/m Boyd Senter, Mel Stitzel.

Carl Ravazza Orchestra: "Vieni Su" (1949), w/m Johnny Cola.

Charlie Agnew Orchestra: "Slow But Sure" (1931), w/m Charlie Agnew, Audree Collins, Charles Newman.

Charlie Straight Orchestra: "Mocking Bird Rag" (1912), w/m Charles T. Straight.

Chuck Foster Orchestra: "Oh, You Beautiful Doll" (1911), w A. Seymour Brown, m Nat D. Ayer.

Del Courtney Orchestra: "Good Evenin'" (1930), w/m Tot Seymour, Charles O'Flynn, Al Hoffman.

Earl Hines Orchestra: "Deep Forest" (1933), w Andy Razaf, m Reginald Foresythe, Earl Hines; "Cavernism" (1935), m Jimmy Mundy, Earl Hines.

Enrico Madriguera Orchestra: "Adios" (1931), w/m Enrico Madriguera, M. Woods, C. R. Del Campo.

Freddie Rich Orchestra: "I'm Always Chasing Rainbows" (1918), w Joseph McCarthy, m Harry Carroll (based on a melody from Frédéric Chopin); "So Beats My Heart for You" (1930), w/m Francis Drake "Pat" Ballard, Charles Henderson, Tom Waring.

Hal McIntyre Orchestra: "Moon Mist" (1942), w/m Mercer Ellington.

Harlan Leonard Orchestra: "Southern Fried" (1940), w/m Harlan Leonard, James Ross, Fred Culliver.

Henry Jerome Orchestra: "Nice People (with Nice Habits)" (1938), w/m Nat Mills, Fred Malcolm.

Johnny Long Orchestra: "In a Shanty in Old Shanty Town" (1932), w Joe Young, m Little Jack Little, John Siras.

Johnny Messner Orchestra: "Can't We Be Friends?" (1929), w Paul James, m Kay Swift.

Les Hite Orchestra: "It Must Have Been a Dream" (1935), w/m Charles Lawrence, Les Hite, Al Stillman, Marv Johnson.

Mike Riley Orchestra: "The Music Goes 'Round and 'Round" (1935), w Red Hodgson, m Edward Farley, Michael Riley.

Orrin Tucker Orchestra: "Drifting and Dreaming" (1925), w Haven Gillespie, m Egbert Van Alstyne, Erwin R. Schmidt, Loyal Curtis.

Paul Tremaine Orchestra: "Lonely Acres" (1926), w/m Willard Robison.

Phil Ohman Orchestra: "Canadian Capers" (1915), w/m Gus Chandler, Bert White, Henry Cohen.

Ray McKinley Orchestra: "Howdy, Friends," w/m Ray McKinley (recorded 1947).

Rudy Vallée Orchestra: "My Time Is Your Time" (1925), w R. S. Hooper, m H. M. Tennant.

Sam Lanin Orchestra: "A Smile Will Go A Long, Long Way" (1923), w/m Benny Davis, Harry Akst.

Smith Ballew Orchestra: "Home" (1931), w/m Harry Clarkson, Peter Van Steeden, Jeff Clarkson (sign-off theme).

Tiny Hill Orchestra: "Angry" (1925), w Dudley Mecum, m Henry Brunies, Jules Cassard, Merritt Brunies.

Bibliography

Belaire, David. *A Guide to the Big Band Era: A Comprehensive Review of All the Recorded Hits and All the Hitmakers.* Santa Ana, CA: Winged Note Press, 1996.

Ewen, David. *All the Years of American Popular Music.* Englewood Cliffs, NJ: Prentice-Hall, 1977.

Feather, Leonard. *The New Edition of the Encyclopedia of Jazz.* New York: Bonanza Books, 1960.

Gammond, Peter. *The Oxford Companion to Popular Music.* Oxford: Oxford University Press, 1991.

Gammond, Peter and Raymond Horricks, eds. *Big Bands.* Cambridge: P. Stephens, 1981.

Kinkle, Roger D. *The Complete Encyclopedia of Popular Music and Jazz, 1900-1950.* New Rochelle, NY: Arlington House, 1974 (four volumes).

Larkin, Colin, ed. *The Guinness Encyclopedia of Popular Music,* Second Edition. Enfield, Middlesex, England: Guinness Publishing, 1995 (six volumes).

Lax, Roger, and Frederick Smith. *The Great Song Thesaurus,* Second Edition. New York: Oxford University Press, 1995.

Lissauer, Robert. *Lissauer's Encyclopedia of Popular Music in America, 1888 to the Present.* New York: Facts on File, 1996 (three volumes).

Morse, Jim. *The Big Band Era.* Hopkins, MN: Hiawatha Publishers, 1991.

Schuller, Gunther. *The Swing Era: The Development of Jazz, 1930-1945.* New York: Oxford University Press, 1989.

Shapiro, Nat, ed. *Popular Music: An Annotated Index of American Popular Songs,* Second Edition. New York: Adrian Press, 1967 (many volumes).

Simon, George Thomas. *The Big Bands,* Fourth Edition. New York: Schirmer, 1981.

Studwell, William E. *The Americana Song Reader.* Binghamton, NY: The Haworth Press, Inc., 1997.

Studwell, William E. *The Popular Song Reader: A Sampler of Well-Known Twentieth-Century Songs.* Binghamton, NY: The Haworth Press, Inc., 1994.

Walker, Leo. *The Big Band Almanac,* Revised Edition. New York: Da Capo Press, 1989.

Person and Group Index

Abbott, Bud, 254
Adams, A. Emmett, 246
Adams, Stanley, 145, 216
Adamson, Harold, 13, 91, 150, 209, 210
Ager, Milton, 49, 163, 201, 211
Agnew, Charlie, 269
Ahlert, Fred E., 16, 19, 85, 163
Akst, Harry, 51, 119, 190, 233, 242, 270
Al Donahue Orchestra, 269
Al King Orchestra, 211
Al Trace Orchestra, 45
Albert Hibbler Orchestra, 228
Albrecht, Elmer, 75, 166
Alden, John, 246
Alexander, Van, 241
Allen, Gracie, 189, 261
Allen, Steve, 20, 155
Allyson, June, 78, 79
Alter, Louis, 12, 14, 146, 190
Altman, Arthur, 67, 84, 145, 206
Alvino Rey Orchestra, 246
American Jazz Orchestra, 225
Amsterdam, Morey, 267
Anderson, Edmund, 65
Anderson, Leroy, 79
Anderson, Maxwell, 129
Andrews Sisters, 7, 8, 83, 119, 157, 265
Andy Kirk Orchestra, 265
Anson Weeks Orchestra, 269
Anthony, Ray, 119, 120, 121, 122, 125
Antonini, Raymond, 121
Anzelwitz, Benjamin, 163
Arias, Clotilde, 267
Arkin, Alan, 172

Arlen, Harold, 17, 27, 121, 156, 157, 168, 170, 190, 198, 246, 247, 257, 258, 267
Armstrong, Louis, 48, 53, 64, 78, 169, 170, 231, 235
Arnaz, Desi, 91, 92, 241
Arndt, Felix, 97, 141
Arnheim, Gus, 190, 237, 238, 239
Arodin, Sidney, 127
Arshawsky, Arthur, 5
Art Hickman Orchestra, 202
Art Jarrett Orchestra, 209
Art Kassell Orchestra, 269
Artie Shaw Orchestra, *xv,* 3, 4, 5, 6
Asaf, George, 238
Ash, Francis, 135
Astaire, Fred, 197
Atkins, Boyd, 36
Auletti, Leonard, 121
Austin, Ray, 173, 187
Ayer, Nat D., 269
Ayres, Mitchell, 253, 254

Baer, Abel, 145, 183
Bailey, Pearl, 231
Baker, Jack, 31
Baker, Phil, 163
Baker, Tafft, 121
Baldridge, Fanny, 9, 214
Ball, Ernest R., 247
Ballard, Francis Drake, 190, 270
Ballard, Pat, 190, 270
Ballew, Smith, 270
Baltimore Symphony Orchestra, 199
Band of Renown, 243
Banks, Marian, 217
Barefield, Eddie, 221

Barnet, Charles Daly, 29
Barnet, Charlie, 29, 31, 92, 191, 255
Barrie, Royden, 84
Barris, Harry, 105, 237
Barron, Blue, 21
Barron, Tony, 179
Barroso, Ary, 216
Bart, Lionel, 128
Bartley, Dallas, 173
Basie, Count, *xv*, 9, 13, 45, 46, 47,
        48, 49, 50, 81, 82, 111, 115,
        221, 223, 224, 231, 239, 255
Basie, William, 47, 221
Bassman, George, 71, 100, 147
Baudac, Ray, 20, 155
Baum, Bernie, 48
Bayes, Nora, 40, 46
Bayha, Charles, 239
Bayly, Thomas Haynes, 77
Beadell, Emily, 126
Bean, Carl, 245
Beck, Morty, 82
Beethoven, Ludwig Van, 64
Belasco, Lionel, 267
Belle, Barbara, 13, 41
Bellis, Hall, 213
Ben Bernie Orchestra, *xv*, 161, 163,
        239
Ben Pollack Orchestra, 211
Beneke, Tex, 78
Benjamin, Bennie, 63, 64, 181
Bennett, Dave, 43
Bennie Krueger Orchestra, 269
Bennie Moten's Kansas City
        Orchestra, 221
Benny, Jack, 234
Benny Carter Orchestra, 223, 225
Benny Goodman Orchestra, 7, 9, 11,
        13, 21, 35, 36, 39, 92, 93,
        158, 214, 234, 235
Benny Meroff Orchestra, 269
Benny Strong Orchestra, 247
Benson, Edgar, 241
Bergen, Edgar, 261
Bergman, Ingrid, 23

Berigan, Bunny, 21, 22, 23
Berigan, Roland Bernard, 21
Berle, Milton, 45
Berlin, Irving, 16, 21, 34, 53, 57,
        112, 149, 180, 209, 212, 213,
        241, 246, 267
Berman, Maurice, 192
Bernabei, Memo, 234
Bernard, Al, 190
Bernie, Ben, *xv*, 49, 104, 161, 162,
        163, 239
Bernier, Buddy, 109, 207
Bernstein, Elmer, 128
Bernstein, Leonard, 119
Berrios, Pedro, 216
Berry, Leon, 233
Bibo, Irving, 204
Bigard, Albany, 57
Billy Butterfield Orchestra, 269
Billy Eckstine Orchestra, 15, 16
Billy May Orchestra, 269
Billy McDonald Orchestra, 39
Billy Strayhorn Orchestra, 227, 228
Biondi, Ray, 65
Bishop, Joe, 44, 158
Bivens, Burke, 213
Bizet, Georges, 175
Blackburn, John, 269
Blake, Eubie, 14, 135, 234
Bloom, Rube, 4, 17, 18, 146
Blue Barron Orchestra, 21
Bob Cats, 19
Bob Crosby Orchestra, 17, 19, 94
Bobby Byrne Orchestra, 269
Bobby Sherwood Orchestra, 269
Bock, Jerry, 64
Bogart, Humphrey, 23
Boland, Clay, 196, 246
Bonine, Joseph, 9, 214
Bonney, Betty, 111
Borelli, Bill, 191
Borodin, Alexander, 62
Bostic, Earl, 67
Boswell Sisters, 54
Boutelje, Phil, 13

Mandel, Mel, 128
Mann, Dave, 64, 67
Mann, Paul, 12, 146
Manne, Joe, 186
Manners, Henry, 34, 212
Manners, Zeke, 267
Manning, Dick, 125
Mantle, Mickey, 111, 112
Marcelino, Muzzy, 209
Marcus, Sol, 64, 181
Markes, Larry, 11, 267
Marks, Gerald, 99
Marsala, Joe, 183
Marsh, Roy K., 204
Martin, Freddy, 171, 172, 173, 187,
    203
Martin, Sam, 45
Marvell, Holt, 247
Marx, Chico, 149
Marx, Groucho, 149
Marx, Gummo, 149
Marx, Harpo, 149
Marx, Zeppo, 149
Marx Brothers, 54, 149
Mason, John, 48
Masters, Frankie, 245
Matthias, Jack, 82
Maxine Sullivan Orchestra, 39
Maxwell, Robert, 7, 22, 113
May, Billy, 269
Mays, Willie, 111, 112
McCarthy, Joseph, 85, 123, 124, 212,
    214, 270
McCartney, Paul, 157, 259
McCoy, Clyde, 43, 44, 50
McDonald, Billy, 39
McGrane, Paul, 75, 81
McHugh, Jimmy, 16, 36, 53, 146,
    167, 170, 190, 210, 229, 264
McIntyre, Hal, 270
McKinley, Ray, 270
McKinley's Cotton Pickers, 222, 231
McKuen, Rod, 245
McMichael, Ted, 182
McRae, Teddy, 6, 35

McVea, Jack, 48
Meacham, Frank W., 77, 78
Mecum, Dudley, 270
Meinken, Fred, 187
Memo Bernabei Orchestra, 234
Mencher, Murray, 211
Mendonca, W. Newton, 128
Menendez, Nilo, 53, 98
Mercer, Johnny, 4, 6, 7, 14, 17, 18, 27,
    52, 59, 60, 63, 73, 79, 99, 112,
    128, 135, 146, 156, 157, 173,
    227, 242, 246, 247, 249, 257,
    267
Meroff, Benny, 213, 269
Meskill, Jack, 161, 162
Messner, Johnny, 270
Meyer, George W., 145
Meyer, Joseph, 12, 13, 238
Meyers, Billy, 14
Mike Riley Orchestra, 270
Miley, B., 55
Miller, Glenn, 3, 61, 63, 70, 71, 72,
    73, 74, 75, 76, 77, 78, 79, 81,
    92, 120, 166, 223
Miller, Sonnie, 179
Mills, Irving, 10, 11, 12, 14, 27, 57,
    71, 93, 221, 225, 228
Mills, Nat, 270
Mills Brothers, 57, 127
Mitchell, Margaret, 183
Mitchell, Sidney D., 14, 49, 105,
    163, 190, 239
Mitchell Ayres and his Fashions in
    Music, 253, 254
Mizzy, Vic, 112
Moll, Billy, 237
Monaco, James V., 85, 123, 124,
    246, 247
Monroe, Vaughn, 64, 91, 92
Moore, Fleecie, 155
Morales, Noro, 216
Moret, Neil, 242
Morey, Larry, 33, 210
Morgan, Russ, 123, 125, 126
Morrow, Buddy, 185

Title Index

Order Your Own Copy of
This Important Book for Your Personal Library!

THE BIG BAND READER
Songs Favored by Swing Era Orchestras and Other Popular Ensembles

_____ in hardbound at $59.95 (ISBN: 0-7890-0914-5)

_____ in softbound at $24.95 (ISBN: 0-7890-0915-3)

COST OF BOOKS_____	☐ **BILL ME LATER:** ($5 service charge will be added)
	(Bill-me option is good on US/Canada/Mexico orders only;
OUTSIDE USA/CANADA/	not good to jobbers, wholesalers, or subscription agencies.)
MEXICO: ADD 20%_____	
	☐ Check here if billing address is different from
POSTAGE & HANDLING_____	shipping address and attach purchase order and
(US: $3.00 for first book & $1.25	billing address information.
for each additional book	
Outside US: $4.75 for first book	
& $1.75 for each additional book)	Signature_____
SUBTOTAL_____	☐ **PAYMENT ENCLOSED: $**_____
IN CANADA: ADD 7% GST_____	☐ **PLEASE CHARGE TO MY CREDIT CARD.**
STATE TAX_____	☐ Visa ☐ MasterCard ☐ AmEx ☐ Discover
(NY, OH & MN residents, please	☐ Diner's Club
add appropriate local sales tax)	
	Account #_____
FINAL TOTAL_____	
(If paying in Canadian funds,	Exp. Date_____
convert using the current	
exchange rate. UNESCO	Signature_____
coupons welcome.)	

Prices in US dollars and subject to change without notice.

NAME _____

INSTITUTION _____

ADDRESS _____

CITY _____

STATE/ZIP _____

COUNTRY _____ COUNTY (NY residents only) _____

TEL _____ FAX _____

E-MAIL_____

May we use your e-mail address for confirmations and other types of information? ☐ Yes   ☐ No

Order From Your Local Bookstore or Directly From
The Haworth Press, Inc.
10 Alice Street, Binghamton, New York 13904-1580 • USA
TELEPHONE: 1-800-HAWORTH (1-800-429-6784) / Outside US/Canada: (607) 722-5857
FAX: 1-800-895-0582 / Outside US/Canada: (607) 772-6362
E-mail: getinfo@haworthpressinc.com

PLEASE PHOTOCOPY THIS FORM FOR YOUR PERSONAL USE.

BOF96